Titl...

Shrouded Blessings

Basil Diki

Langaa Research & Publishing CIG
Mankon, Bamenda

Publisher:
Langaa RPCIG
Langaa Research & Publishing Common Initiative
Group
P.O. Box 902 Mankon
Bamenda
North West Region
Cameroon
Langaagrp@gmail.com
www.langaa-rpcig.net

Distributed outside N. America by African Books
Collective
orders@africanbookscollective.com
www.africanbookscollective.com

Distributed in N. America by Michigan State
University Press
msupress@msu.edu
www.msupress.msu.edu

ISBN: 9956-616-07-9

DISCLAIMER

The names, characters, places and incidents in this book are either the product of the author's imagination or are used fictitiously. Accordingly, any resemblance to actual persons, living or dead, events, or locales is entirely one of incredible coincidence.

Contents

Act Three

Act Four

Appendice

Author's Notes & Glossary

Preface

I am profoundly indebted to the following people: my sister Molly Diki for material support during the research and writing of this work; Cuthbert Matengaifa for complementing my sister's effort; Dread Johannes Phiri of Gwarimbo Street for moral support; the humble mystic Tauya Mandla from the Harare Sat Sang who rekindled my desire for self-realisation in the early 90s with whom I've unfortunately lost touch with ever since; Sheik Jula ba'Adam of the Rimuka Islamic Mosque for diligently taking me through a year-long tutorial of the Quran in 1992; the family's sworn undertaker-cum-preacher, my nephew Rev Phibion Mupingiza, whose biblical utterances reminded me of my mortality and urged me to write fervently at a time when my health was failing. But before illness could interrupt the thirty-one-day drafting and writing of Shrouded Blessings, beginning 15 April, 2009, my good friend Stanford Chipungu took it upon himself to see to it that my health was mended. With the same depth of sincerity, I am also grateful to my wife, Joleen, my family and siblings for according me the quiet and solitude I needed to write this story.

I am equally indebted to Rabbi Aharon ben Shimon* (PhD) of the Centre for Jewish (Hasidic) Studies, Warsaw, who put together Appendix I. He also provided the translated version of the cabbalistic passage in the ancient Babylonian Talmud, *Hagigah* 14b, for clarity and insight to aid readers not familiar with Talmudic teachings and the Cabbala, and briefly commented on the passage vis-à-vis the story, confining his brief analysis to Act Two, Scene One. I'm humbled by the fact that the Professor went out of his way to assist me. Those in the know will attest to the fact that rabbis, like many mystics, tend to be reticent about their own mystical experiences and knowledge, and that Judaism is rarely expounded to Gentiles. The learned man spared time to explain the exoteric and esoteric elements of the Torah, delving into the Zohar and other cabbalistic works, out of which I gleaned invaluable hidden knowledge to blend into this story.

I acknowledge and appreciate the cooperation of Mr Rutledge Davis [†], a high-ranking official of the Buddhist Society of London, for further demystifying Buddhist elements of the story, elucidating my Buddhist poem of Act Three, Scene Three by simplifying the glossary. Appendix I and the Buddhist terms in the Notes and Glossary will aid non-Jewish and/or non-Buddhist readers whose lack of exposure to such ancient teachings and their writings could impede their comprehension of the story. These endeavours were intended to afford the readers a better understanding of the fictionalised Talmudic passage and the essence of Buddhism to enhance their enjoyment of the story. Reproduction of the Hagigah (14b) was also intended to avoid any corruption of the sacred passage that would cause offence in Jewish circles.

For the National Anthem of South Africa (Appendix II) and South African ethnic terms used in the story, I am indebted to some friendly staff members of the High Commission of South Africa in Harare, whom I consulted for words and their meanings, although they did not realise I was an author enquiring after the arcana of their diversified and rich cultures. Their names I withhold because I did not formally seek their assistance through their High Commissioner, an emissary I preferred not to importune when I could achieve the object of my desire by other means. For the Nigerian words used I wish to thank Nigerian businessmen in Harare, especially at the Gulf, who proudly offered me a Yoruba vocabulary and an understanding of a few of their 1700 deities. The businessmen, like the deities, are too numerous to mention.

While the Roman Catholic Cathedral of Christ the King is in central Johannesburg and many places named in the story including the Vatican are manifestly real and de facto, all the characters, except names identified historically, are fictitious and not based on any dead or living persons. However, the story is an eruption from a statement of fact by some girl of about sixteen years to her nephew, Chenjerai Zinoro, who was my workmate about twelve years ago before his emigration to Scotland. The girl revealed to Chenjerai that she was dating and obsessed with elderly men. I'm thankful to him for expressing his shock to me.

Any errors in this work are mine alone.

✳ A pseudonym of the Rabbi's preference

† A witty close corruption of the Buddhist's name

Basil Diki, Kadoma

CHARACTERS

Father Bryn Flynn	Roman Catholic priest, Irish.
Naomi Ngqawane	A teenage Xhosa enchantress
Bonginkosi	A young Zulu entrepreneur
Sogo Sogo	An African male tramp
Sigcawu Mangcotywa	An elderly Sangoma (spirit medium)
Rabbi Hayyim ben Avuyah	A Jewish Cabbalist
Cardinal Duccio Pietro di Niccolo	A Roman Catholic Cardinal, Italian

Plus:

Two white mass Servers

Six Roman Cardinals

Two ceremonious Vatican guards

Vincent   A six-year old coloured boy

A rural male teenager

Two middle-aged rustic Xhosa men

1

Act One

SCENE ONE

Sunday morning
Pulpit of the Roman Catholic Cathedral of Christ the King, Johannesburg

Curtain opens to reveal the altar half-laden with the requisite silver Eucharist appointments. Crimson, emerald-green and gold light from stained glass floods the pulpit. Six unlit candles are arranged symmetrically on elevated stands on either side of the altar; three on one side, three on the other. Low worshipful Catholic choral music pervades from outside the Cathedral. Enter two white SERVERS in white robes, one carrying a tray of silverware and the other a corked wine bottle on a smaller tray, which they solemnly place on the altar. One arranges the appointments while the other uncorks the bottle and pours its contents into the chalice. Both step back and genuflect. Exit in single file the two, their hands clasped prayerfully. Enter SOGO SOGO from the opposite direction, carrying a cumbersome load of bric-a-brac on his back. Pausing briefly, he looks about on the pulpit and then places his load near the altar. With priestly mien, he stands behind the altar, opens the chalice and sets the lid on the altar.

Sogo
(*Examining the wine in the chalice*)

Is this the sacred blood or a hoax for the remembrance?

Was the essence in the blood or in the remembrance?

In the Book of Ezekiel are images appearing like creatures

Of incense he wrote not, but of imagination and reverence.

When I look at it, the account is suggestive of elusiveness

And the satanic suggestion is averse to scriptures.

Of the throne, he talks of the likeness of a throne.
Likeness versus image, logic and reason injures.
Of appearance, he says with the likeness of a sapphire
stone.
He who attains immortality in the heavens is he who
endures.
Of the likeness and appearance of the sapphire-stone
throne
He says, was upon it the likeness as the appearance
of a man.
And upon these, was the likeness of the appearance
of glory.
The Pacer's empire surpasses manifold vast and lost
Ottoman
The Treaty of Versailles found favour and halted gory
To the One pray I without ceasing, reason or season
For I am nothing founded on appearance in an allegory.
(Looks upwards, but for a while marvels at the beams of colourful light)
O God, is poverty liberty with the likeliness of
poverty?
Is life, life; suffering, suffering; adversity, adversity?
But this phenomenon of appearances was moving,
So are we though groping bats and trudging weaklings,
So are the continents, so are the roving constellations.
Bless the wine, fruit of the vine, True Vine of all
creations.
Father of spirits, in this jihad in bewildering darkness
Am I a shadow, an appearance or animated blankness?
In this unyielding wilderness of masquerades,
Am I the likeliness of an appearance of a man?
Blindness shrouds my thoughts and my faculties
barricades.
Free will is the cause of our doing evil, so Oxford
teaches.
Your just dictatorship our suffering evil, your Word
preaches.

The oesophagus to my oblongata is sore from
propaganda
Spare me from doctrines of death that besieged
Uganda.
O this is Paul come to a philosophers' void Areopagus
Neither rider of a decorated horse nor the mighty
Pegasus
But on white wine distilled like rays of the sun
stumbles
Yet on its pebbles, hearer or no hearer, the apostle
ambles.
To Thee draw me nearer, there being nothing else to say.
O! How can a thinking mind have reason to be sad
On this momentous and newfound brand new day
Not organdie human hands but *Adonai* has made?
Angels, servants of man, help me jamboree in jubilee.
The order of events in the order of the ordained
disorder
Wasn't an offspring of anarchy and chaos mating in a
melee
But is an anaconda than the foundations of the earth
older.

(*With both hands he lifts the chalice overhead. Voice cathedral*)

Through Your divine goodness I have this wine to
offer;
Fruit of the vine and product of human endeavour.
Spirit begotten of Spirit, Primordial Drifter, Rover
Decree the wine sacrament for my serpentine
manoeuvre
Over me, may Your deathless spirit and grace forever
hover.

*Brings chalice to his lips and drinks greedily, recklessly, some wine
spilling from the sides of his mouth. Enter the two SERVERS,
carrying more appointments. They freeze in shock on seeing Sogo,
who sets the chalice down and grins.*

1st Server

(To 2nd Server)

What do we have on our hands?
A man without his faculties or the Tempter?

(Appraises Sogo theatrically then addresses him in jocular fashion)

By appearance a vagrant, a vagabond attested.
By his dire presence the Return stands arrested.
Could this be the Eater of souls, the Tormentor,
Of persecutors, philosophers and atheists mentor;
Of whom it is written by his hand man tasted death?
Is what stands before us a representative of sounder?
What thou camest to do, do quickly like Peter Fonda.
Cast the universal suffrage into that dreaded hearth.
Spice and sacrilege Communion into pig's fodder
Herald the end of times and the folding of the earth.

Sogo

I'm an epistle of words broadcasting wisdom, Amen.
The Holy Writ Zoë that whisks mankind from doom.
I'm a ray of light sent to dispel the darkness in man.
I'm a billboard of epaulets, forerunner to the Kingdom.
As an ambassador extraordinaire jeopardise I nothing.
I'm a man of laurels in letters and pursuer of knowledge
When He sent the twelve yonder, lacked they anything?
Acknowledge that ignorance entombs and is not a privilege.

1st Server

For all intents and purposes I'm non-racial,
But it looks like you are of no fixed abode,
A societal nuisance Satan deprived of leeway,
A nonentity of nothing and nowhere special.
It breaks my heart to be the one to turn you away.
I take it that it pleases God that you take your leave.

Sogo

God is not a man to enjoy pleasure or suffer
displeasure.
To liken God to men is the vilest of sins beyond
remission
Is it not written that all sins shall be forgiven mankind;
Except sins against the Spirit, which are sins against man?
The winch of the Spirit shall drag both saints and
witches.
Know that by perusing the scriptures you lose nothing.
Watch lest on the day you wilt from the foretold
gnashing.
Your wits dare use, but only towards your
disinheritance.
The Holy Writ was deftly written for continuous
perusal
That divine wisdom takes over our minds at
repentance.
But life you deny yourselves with your strenuous
refusal.
From the mesmerising cleavages of women dorsal-
fin deep
Like pimps you see a glimpse of heaven thus doze
with sleep.

2nd Server

(*To fellow* Server)

Reason with the Devil to your spiritual detriment.
In his captivations and mesmerising tendencies
His renderings, disguises and calculated utterances
Are a logical impairment that scriptures defy.
The Spirit my edifier, like Paul myself I magnify
The Devil ejaculates words that turn the gospel
algebraic
His brilliance at coercion and obligation the soul injures.
Belief and logic sit ill together, a fact most archaic.
Apt at arresting your passage, anything he endures.

Sogo

By deliberately avoiding to reason you therefore reason.
Know you not that eyes craving sleep drive away sleep?
Reason not, but offer your body as a living sacrifice;
Suffice to say, which is your only reasonable service.
Beware the mouth is to a dark catacomb an orifice
Whose province it is to make or unmake its owner
Or, like a gladiator, your life with zeal you dishonour.

1st Server

Calamity and death
You invite by your undesirable presence near the altar.
As an ark shall this laden altar stand before us all.
Let not these appointments, blessed as they now stand
Depart from their anointment and cast you into the
hearth.
Sniff the air, already cast into it plumes of incense.
For now God's attention is arrested on a spot on Earth
Therefore speaker, intruder, time is of the essence,
Convince us you are not in the Devil's confederacy.

Sogo

The god-sent you liken to the Devil.
Think scripturally and answer not in insults.
I consent to the Word and do not suffer evil
For I know the world is a pendulum fraught
With draughts of perambulating spiritual bandits.
Earth, a bridge, reels from an enlightenment drought.
The habitual who build houses on it find it an anvil.
The grace of God stands sentinel over my soul.
Submit I this to you: like a restless weevil
Search the scriptures; that is my advice sole.

2nd Server

Pray as a matter of urgency.
Petition God to disentangle you from the Devil's spell
And bestow you the inheritance of your regency
The Devil scouts for prey to descend with into hell.

Sogo

The Dead Sea scrolls were discovered and deciphered.
Daily you read and their verses commit to memory
But astoundingly you fail to see beyond the words.
On them is it written: whip till he howls and yelps,
He who, like a smelting furnace brick, thirsts?
Or he who, like the sheltering Samaritan, helps
God by quenching the desert's sweltering weary?
He who rescues the beggar from starvation by giving
alms,
Disregarder of self and his dearest and grasper of
Psalms,
Pall bearer of paupers and surrogate father to all
orphans,
Bringer of hope to those pinioned by steadfast
obstacles,
He who barnacles the condemned on a brimstone
oven,
Is he not the never-shortened hand of the Heavens?
For God has no members and uses our hands often.
And you, Athenian residues, in all things superstitious!
In the abode between the firmaments *persona non-grata*,
Open your eyes to he who sleeps in thistles and the
gutter.
The beggar clothing the archangel Gabriel, embrace.
With humility and reverence bow to the stigmata.
Only love and discipleship will that wound dress.
Behold, I come to you in the name of able *Qamata*.

2nd Server

(Impatiently, gesturing towards the exit with finality)

Force and vile words are with vehemence forbidden
Lest the adamant stoic old man buried and forgotten
Should rear his ugly head again and mar righteousness.
The maxim of our faith is the maintenance of holiness
Upholding cleanliness which is next to godliness

11

And perforce meekness that borders on sheepishness
Sir, solicitously we ask; take out your filthy baggage.
God's hands are not tied to curtail your permissiveness
To engage force is injurious to our faith and bondage.

Sogo

(*Picks bundle*)

Said I gently: I come to you in the name of the Lord.
But belligerently in the house of the Lord you rage.
Unlike the genteel sages of old, with anger you surge.
Is this the end-time foolishness of vengeance for God?
Benighted fools darkening an already dark Africa!
Needlessly you bedevil yourselves with Samuel's spirit
God is the Primordial Truth, therefore indivisible.
Your assumed piety does not render Him deceivable.
Our Lord is not limp though limbless and invisible.
This good God is not the conceivable and ageless
aBantu bomlambo, despite their deathlessness,
From the roaring Limpopo River and the endless
Indian Ocean and its immeasurable limitlessness.
Nor is He stoppable like the conquerable *impundulu.*
This God is more ferocious than the demons of the Zulu.

1st Server

With words we haggle and scuffle to no avail.
Your presence rends again the temple's veil.

Sogo

(*Starting towards the exit*)

Beware, you of floppy minds, of the folly of disbelief,
I came not to hobble before men but to give you relief.
Count everything that happens under the sun a blessing.
Sit back and before long you shall notice in awe
That veritably all and sundry, demons and angels
Work like greased clockwork in ministering to all.

Having made myself plain, my priceless duty to
mankind,
My leave I take, but seek none from my pilgrimage.
Though like a hippopotamus I lumber in this mirage
My words to man are grace and to me heavenly
mileage
Accept my bidding you farewell, servers of lame
lineage
Pray I, givers of the remembrance, may God save us.

Exit SOGO. *The Servers shake their heads, sigh and cross to the
altar. They set on it the appointments they brought. With white cloths
they wipe the altar and the floor where the wine fell. One of them
takes the chalice. Both step back and genuflect in unison. Exit the
Servers in single file again.*

Enter FR BRYN FLYNN *from the direction of* SOGO'S *exit.
The priest is in full Eucharist regalia; a striking chasuble, stole, alb
and amice. He is reading a printed letter and shaking his head ruefully.
He pauses at the altar, gazing absent-mindedly at the appointments
before he folds the letter and tucks it away in his cincture. Assuming
piety, he crosses himself and genuflects towards the altar, then kneels
in prayer.*

Fr. Flynn

(*Praying*)

Almighty, my guilt and shame are immeasurable.
Despite my reverence, Heaven unknowable,
I was as despicable as mother-and-son incest.
Cynically, I disgraced the heavenly declaration,
Which clinically states in solemnity and in truth
That he in whom You dwell is not overtaken by sin.
Seer of every scene, in realms seen and worlds unseen
What can I do to mortify my flesh? I breached
Without shame my vow of chastity. Yet I preached
The Word though backslidden and of mind gross,
And dangerously void of heavenly gloss.
O God incorruptible! This night of mine!

13

This self-inflicted and scalding Gethsemane!
Pray I that you, Lord immutable, abstract me from it.
Now on account of my mortal sins, the Holy See
Has subpoenaed me. Word, Instigator of earth and sea
Of heaven and earth, the known and the unknown, Initiator
That which ear cannot hear nor eye see, Originator
Cast from your presence I become a beleaguered torso
But if I descend into Hell certainly Thou art there also.
Alpha and Omega, quell forever my burning libido,
Which erupts like sparks, consigning my soul to limbo
O sin! Thou art a boomerang. Upon the water I cast you
But being a demon returned to haunt me with aggression.
Neither high up mountains nor deep in gulfs of carnality
Can a mortal man hide from Your anger. Holy Sanctity,
Ought I to repent in sackcloth and be smeared in ashes?
Where can I submit myself for forty-minus-one lashes?
(He pauses hesitantly and continues in a slightly hushed voice)
Master of Judgment Day, my eyes were my undoing.
Had I been born blind I wouldn't have impregnated her;
On her voluminous assets and almond eyes my eyes rested.
I confess a married woman my fear of You arrested.
Yet upon your name denied it I categorically. This devilment,
Thanks to the husband, a simpleton who bowed to riches,
Accepted money and was game to an out-of-court settlement
Was tailored against Heaven to catapult a priest from light.

14

By not guiding against the devil's machinations I
sinned.

In darkness I had surrendered my miniature sceptre
as surety.

This sceptre, a unique gift from the hands of the
Archbishop

With its INRI, spiralling squiggles and delicate
curlicues,

O gracious Redeemer, is an Italian marvellous rarity.

Clandestinely and in cahoots, the woman and I, Father,

Cows to the slaughterer, for delivery loomed,
connived

Dreading the calamitous effects of an agreed paternity test.

Darkness begot darkness; she perished in the delivery
position

In a makeshift dank theatre, a victim of a botched
abortion.

Against me forensic evidence was developed and is
mounted

For neither reason nor gain save to destroy and to harm.

Foremost the blood-type then the irrefutable genetic
proof,

Then the mini-sceptre found lodged deep in her
womb,

Supposedly taken in faith to the backyard theatre as
a charm,

Upon my sworn word, Lord, she would the ordeal
survive.

The autopsy established a perforated diaphragm and
a lung.

Arraigned, the abortionist pleaded drunkenness and
insanity.

But I thank you Lord; he mentioned me not as an
accomplice.

Now the post-mortem and forensic reports are in the
Vatican,

Together with the sceptre the Archbishop positively
identified.
I pray that Your rectitude shall prevail over men's
edict.
If Thou art unforgiving, to what avail then was the
Lamb slain?
In You graciousness abounds, O let Your Word be
the verdict.
Excommunication or disrobing renders crucifixion vain.
The resplendent Seven-hilled city, work of human
hands,
Iridescent, proud, glorious and awe-inspiring as it
stands
Is a miniature of a minute miniature on Your
footstool.
Come hail, come thunder, I dare remain a heavenly tool.

Enter NAOMI. *Her face is overdone with make-up. She is trendy
in a long, figure-hugging skirt that sweeps the floor, a matching
sleeveless blouse and expensive bracelets and necklaces. A trendy
purse is clasped under her arm. Kneeling a few paces behind him, she
crosses herself and coughs to attract his attention.* FR FLYNN
turns and looks at her.

Naomi

(*Feigning shyness*)
    Excuse me, Father, but over a year ago was my last
    confession.
    You love and shepherd the flock without subjection
    to passion.
    Pray I, Father, grant me a few minutes before the
    procession.

Fr Flynn rises and appraises her.

Fr. Flynn

(*Glances at his wrist watch*)
    Expedient it must be, lass;
    Michael's quiver is never devoid of arrows.

16

My daughter, be informed, nothing delays Mass.
Two copper coins is the price of five sparrows.
In His routine teachings thus taught the Son begotten
Bringing peace to multitudes and drowning all sorrows
Yet none of the sparrows before God is forgotten.
Know that you are dearer than a flock of sparrows.

Naomi

How to put it to you, Reverent Father, I know not.
If I don't, then demonic I am and in hell will rot.
But I'm glad you're a man of God, not Bruce Lee.
In my mind are frightening medleys and a melee
Teenage wisdom and strangling indecision war.
If my feelings prevail then I'll become a whore.

Fr. Flynn

It appears your soul is in mortal danger.
Speak, my daughter, soon the bell will toll.

Naomi

Shoulder my tremendous guilt, Reverent Father.
I shudder to inform you that I seduced my godfather
Innumerably and wantonly and with morbid
resignation.
I defiled his matrimonial bed and destroyed his family.
Have mercy on me, Reverent Father, I sinned against
God.

Fr. Flynn
(Gapes, then whistles softly in disbelief)

Holy Mary! Despicable! A sin most cynical and mortal!
What horrible sacrilege of heart! A requiem scherzo!
What a horrendous showcase of sexual perversion!
What shrubbery-shredding audacity from a minor!
A delicate beauty of ruthless delicatessen features!
Yet you court for yourself a featureless opacity for a
future.

(Heavenward)

Let this not be a condensed evil omen for me.

17

Naomi

My soul suffers bastardisation;
A victim of hell-bent flesh and a foul imagination.
Intercede and end this voyage of mine to destruction.
At baptism I stopped swearing and masturbation.
Foolishly I thought I was rooted in the sure Word
Yet within carnal feelings raged; I was in a shell.
The Evil One's hosts routed my born-again self
Resurrecting my old person bent on fornication.
In my heart I feel I'm on a shuttle, destination – hell

Fr. Flynn

Your confession remorselessly condescends my calling;
Such a ballerina-beauty but a painful cadenza of death!
Why the devil do you candidly put a priest to shame!

(NAOMI *begins to sob. She draws a handkerchief from her purse,* FR FLYNN *looking down at her and shaking his head.*)

But be of good cheer, little girl, you're redeemable;
No soul, no matter how belittled by sin, is irreclaimable.
Upon broadcast some grains fell on rocks and ceded their life.
But, thank God, your confession makes you salvageable seed.
In heaven the Lamb ceaselessly intercedes for his priests.
Who is before me now on whose behalf I must intercede?

Naomi

(*Rises and suddenly collects herself. She drops him a curtsey*)

Frankly, I am a libidinous schoolgirl aged sixteen,
A baptised and confirmed Roman Catholic Xhosa.
Traditional name: Nondwe Sonwabile Ngqawane,
Born on the rolling lollipop-smiling plains of the Cape.
Poppies amid weeds grew, and I was raised on abuse.

Daughter to Thobeka and father Ngquku Ngqawane.
Thobeka my loving mother, a true Xhosa, wasn't obtuse.
When I was thirteen they perished after eating a toadstool.
The memory of Ngquku raises bile in me; it doesn't amuse.
Thank *Qamata* I couldn't partake; I was at a day school.

Fr. Flynn

I'm sorry about your parents, my beloved daughter
This earth is no Eden or mere orchard for laughter.
But departure of parents is not a visa for promiscuity.
At this juncture you need the truth without ambiguity.
In this parish, from Lombardy East to Modderfontein,
From Emmarentia, right across the city, to Turffontein,
Young orphans deeming themselves favoured abound
But these did not bury their self-worth with their parents.
This ugly abomination pierces the hearts of sacred saints.
Since1960, when this great monument was built, hitherto,
A godfather and a godchild have never compromised so.

Naomi

Father, I present myself to be rid of evil sexual intent
That stoically caresses restraint till it dies down like a fire.
Before it became a ravine it was an unnoticeable dent –
A back-of-the mind desire to watch hardcore pornography.
By the day this carnally necessary evil ebbed higher –
A firefly glow turned into a sulphur and brimstone catastrophe.
Runaway feelings give me an estrangement from self.

19

Like anaesthesia they arrest my ability to contain
myself.
I long to be marooned forever with morbid rapists.
Now that I have bared myself to you this obsession
ends
Whose summit is expiring at the hands of erotic
orgiasts.
Frankly, I think I am sexually rabid or I harbour a
demon.
Like a nuclear submarine engine it propels me from
within.
But my subconscious tells me this sweetness is lemon.
But like a carnal screensaver the Devil obstructs
reason.
Forgive me for appearing like the seed that fell on
thorns.

Fr. Flynn

Take it that a confession is not tantamount to treason.
Intercede for you I must, but your names are
jawbreakers.
The mind, spirited, its modus operandi facts and
reason,
Is the abode for the Evil One and his host of spirit-
wreckers.

Naomi

Selfishly, expatriate teachers reasoned and called me
Naomi.
They said I looked like a centrefold model posing in
the nude.
I look back in anger; the name was plucked from a
magazine.
Perhaps the name rouses inherent promiscuity and is
provoking.

Fr. Flynn

Lend ear, further take it that the All-Powerful One
Who desires man to walk on the straight and narrow,

He Himself strait-jacketed in His own hallowedness,
Is by nature powerless to defy His deified Word
Word begotten of Word, Spirit un-begotten and limitless,
Love ever lengthening, deepening and unfolding,
Like the petals of a budding jasmine, captivating
From whose vineyard nothing can estrange us,
He being our sovereign God, of order, the Lord
Is incapable of being with man forever bitter.
But in the cathedral I will not allow superstitious statements.
Roused, God's vinegary rage requires no arbiter.
As His representative I cannot condone vulgar testaments.

Naomi

(*Running her hands over her midsection, her face contorted*)
An invisible demonic screen shades my view.
I crave threesome orgies and scrumptious fellatio.
I drool at orang utan-built men in number few.
Harboured in me are light and darkness in equal ratio.
Whether partaking of communion or sitting on a pew,
Meditating on the trinity or being romanced in the patio,
In rain, sun-drenched beaches or on grass sodden with dew
I fantasise about sex with C.S. Forester's Hornblower Horatio

Fr. Flynn

O! What're you talking about, child?
Wickedness founded on wickedness!
Seemingly a floribunda, yet a toxic orchid!

Naomi

Something agitates my loins beyond my control
In truth and in spirit I am a nonentity feeble
Therefore I'm vulnerable and to stop it unable.

21

In my groin it crawls and crawls like termites.
To elderly businessmen I become vulnerable.
I am more reprehensible than the Sodomites.
Lads my age I find nauseating and full of pretence.
I love and desire elderly men with a passion;
I can be in a man's hands for nothing but a pittance.
The fiend in me is in many girls like some fashion.

Fr. Flynn

(*Heavenward*)

O God, look down in pity.
I confessed and Thou forgave my iniquity.
O! Against fallen angels Thou art her security.
She comes in humility, Alpha and Omega
To be cleansed of vulgar demonic vanity.
Salvage her from evil and urge her to chastity.

(*To her*)

Intercede for you I will, but the root of your debauchery
I must know, lest I prune the leaves and rejuvenate the birch-tree.
You sound wise and well-read beyond your years to repel all evil.
Erudite for one so young, yet against the devil can't claim victory.
Frankly, what comes into your mind when you see a man like me?

Naomi

(*Suddenly breathing heavily*)

You're a hanging garden,
Splendid to look at, yet beyond that, a white elephant.
In fact I'm neither a saint nor a maiden.
Do not reckon me a breast-suckling infant.

(*Sensuously*)

I die to smooch those broad shoulders.

(*Sternly*)

Allow me to touch those robed, muscled boulders.

Gifted to pleasure men, I promise you the time of
your life.

Fr. Flynn

(*Astounded*)

O Diana incarnate from the lost city of Ephesus!
You walk into the cathedral to rob me of my Jesus!

Naomi

Father, stone not Mary, neither consign her to a
dungeon.
I am not liturgical, but vituperation isn't Catholic.
The Church condemns not; it doesn't rebuke or
bludgeon.

Fr. Flynn

Excuse me; you violated my sensibilities.
Your proposal was evil and dangerous to my calling.
By appearance you seem vulnerable like origami
Yet you callously crucify Christ again, Naomi.
When your mouth opens, out springs anomy.
I ruffled you, but the last thing in here is a scuffle.
Today I have grasped the crux of a simple lesson
Which, coming from God, is a delightful soufflé:
In matters spiritual a man ought not to reason.
Though enamoured of sin, you remain a child of God.

*Cathedral bell tolls momentarily. Father Flynn looks at his wrist
watch.*

Your soul is at risk until I intercede for you, lass
I invite you to the confessional after Mass.
Rapturous lust seems your supreme Pharaoh.
Muster restrain I should, lest I indulge or the sheep
devour.
Caution I you: In the interim partake not of the
communion
Or Heaven you would outrage, and your mortal self
pinion.
Presently I'll appraise the set appointments,

23

As prescribed in the Holy Writ on behalf of Christ,
The True Light which gives light to every man,
Indeed my priestly duty to man and God.
Outside in humility and of one accord,
The praise and worship procession,
In piety, loftily raises hallowed banners and ensigns
And at this appointed hour my presence awaits.
My witness and master Christ,
Nothing stays the anointed Eucharist.

Naomi

Yes, Father. Look forward to a full confession.
This unholy alliance of light and darkness within me
This reminiscence of the renowned Passover syndication,
Which, like a tumbling river in flood, has no medication
Comes now and again like qualms —without provocation.
Confess I must lest my soul be forfeited to the Devil.

Enter the two SERVERS, *one carrying the chalice, which he sets on the altar.* NAOMI *crosses herself, genuflects and crosses herself again. Exit* NAOMI. *The* SERVERS *light the candles on holders.* FR FLYNN *crosses to the altar and inspects the set appointments. The three of them genuflect towards the altar. Exit the three as a surge of choral music fills the Cathedral.*

Curtain

SCENE TWO

Sunday afternoon
Inside the confessional stall at the Johannesburg
Catholic Cathedral

SOGO SOGO *is fast asleep on the floor and snoring lightly in the priest's booth, the cumbersome bundle beside him. The confessor's booth is empty. Both booths are dimly lit. Enter* NAOMI *in hipster pants and a navel-revealing blouse. She carries a different purse, all her items trendy. She gets into the booth, closes the door and sits on the bench.* SOGO *doesn't stir and continues to snore.*

Naomi
(*Timidly*)
> Father, I have come to confess my sins.

No response.
(*Louder*)
> Father, I have come to confess my sins!

Sogo wakes with a jerk and sits on the bench in his booth.
Sogo
(*In an assumed British accent; voice priestly*)
> Dying, He descended into death and slaughtered death.
> Rising, He ascended to Heaven and gave impetus to life.
> Child, conceding one baptism for the forgiveness of sins
> All your mortal sins of commission and omission confess.

From an opening in his baggage he draws a loaf of bread and munches gluttonously, tearing the bread with his hands.
Naomi
> Father, I defiled my godfather.

Sogo

(*Wolfing the bread*):
 Go ahead, child.

Naomi

I harbour a tyrannical penchant to bed elders.
I labour fervently against carousing with mature men.
I date them without cruelty but also without pity.
Ply I businessmen with the voracity of a Tsarist pogrom.
Full-grown men find I resounding models for the universe.

Sogo

Is it by the authority of foul spirits or sheer vanity, child?

Naomi

My python endearments are myriad and hypnotising.
In parenthesis, a versatile intelligence is master key.
The emphasis being strictly no kvass, cognac or whisky
A figure pristinely athletic and porcelain-smooth skin
Laughter coy and a bearing of diva-permissiveness;
Add to this quotations from Lincoln, Gandhi and Trotsky.
Effortlessly converse I on global warming, the Al Qaeda,
Osama, Amon Goeth, meteoric Obama and Oskar Schindler.
I am an astounding contrast to the sulking laconic house wife.
Fastened in heartless postures my sadistic prey confess,
Every man saying his wedded wife is an awful bore-
Ever-pregnant, psalm-reading, crocheting or kneading dough.
In one breath men hate and venerate my irresistible charms.

26

Homes I have wrecked and wretchedness on them
wrought
But to the hearts of onanists joy carnal I have brought.

Sogo

Child, ask the Father in Heaven for complete
forgiveness.
God's abode is full of Amazons of eternal
compassion.
It overflows with Euphrateses of mercy and Niles of
gentleness.
Taught the seers of the past: Aversion, confusion and
passion
Are the three fires that burn within with a
relentlessness.

Naomi

Father, *child* you keep calling me impersonally.
This assumed coldness and unaffectionate reference
Is a far cry from the Naomi-aficionado of the morning.
I'm nostalgic for the passionate pronouncement before
Mass.
May I demand to know the priest I am confessing to?

Sogo

The great I'M;
The Rider of Ezekiel's Chariot and of the Four Winds;
The sole Proprietor of the Seven Spirits; God
Almighty.

NAOMI *rises, perplexed. She peers through the knitted opening
into the priest's booth and screams. Exit Naomi in a huff.* SOGO
laughs raucously and continues to eat the bread.

Enter FR FLYNN *confounded by the laughter emanating from the
booth. He is in a two-piece executive suit and a priest's collar.
Crossing himself, he opens the door of the booth cautiously as
SOGO'S laughter dies. The two men stare at each other, the priest
stunned.*

Wrong booth, mortal. Go to the other side for
confession, son.

Fr. Flynn

(*Infuriated*)
> What! Excuse me! I am the vicar, vagrant!
> Out! I order you this instant, or I call the police.
> Devilishly, you force my tongue to turn braggart.
> I heard your wicked hands touched the chalice.

Sogo

(*In his normal voice and accent*)
> Father, be merciful to a peaceful ragamuffin.
> Thus you might entertain an angel, God Argus.
> I beg you not to put my body in a stone coffin.
> This cathedral with its beauty is a sarcophagus.

Fr. Flynn

A drawn-out argument with you I won't entertain.
Alms-givers abound on Nuggert Street, go out and gain.
The niche for beggars is by the entrance in the rain
If not, then, as written, by the roadside in the drain.

Sogo

Silver I cannot seek from a man committed to poverty.
Ask I: upon His Second Coming will He be Djibouti,
A bow-and-arrow Kalahari San or a necktie Englishman?
Are space dare-devils going to see Him ahead of us all?
Will the New Jerusalem, this iridescent, splendid City,
Be in Old Jerusalem or in Harlem shall this Jerusalem be?
Who will prayer-fund the golem that will stop the feuding
Between the adamant Israelis and unyielding Palestinians
That threatens permanent shelving of the Second Coming?
I foresee scholars grown tired of waiting making a U-turn

Rewriting the New Testament and erasing the Return.
They will write about the return of Pharaoh's vermin;
The sad resurrection of Hitler, Saddam and Ida Armin.

SOGO *rises, picks up his bundle and walks wearily towards the exit, Father Flynn watching him go and shakes his head. Exit* SOGO.

Enter BONGINKOSI *after a moment. He is in expensive designer clothes and carrying a leather duffel bag on his back. He walks into the confessor's booth, sets the bag down and sits on the bench.*

Bonginkosi
Father, I am a teensy-weensy bit tormented.
Murderous hurly-burly overshadows my life.
My mind is reeling, soon I might be demented.

Fr. Flynn
Confess your sins, my son; He is ready to absolve them.

Bonginkosi
(*Teary*)

By no hand of mine brought I this hideous calamity.
This castigatory, torturous and murderous sequel,
Which personal prayer and fasting failed to quell.
O Almighty in the Heavens! Why do I suffer so?

Fr. Flynn
My son, the ears of God are open. I say refrain
From using this facility as a lamentation chamber.
No matter that your guilty is piercing, your sin scarlet,
From hearkening to overwrought emotions always abstain.

Bonginkosi
Your patience I sincerely beg.
My father, begetter of seventeen children, died two years ago.
A goal-getter and an entrepreneurial doyen he was;
Restaurateur and proprietor of a casino and cafeterias.

A black granite magnate, partial owner of the Drakensberg,
Ever giving to orphanages in Kimberley and Johannesburg,
Bloemfontein and Pietermaritzburg, in charity he had no rival
Precisely why he was celebrated like the Cannes Film Festival.

Fr. Flynn

This is surely an erroneous submission of a delayed eulogy.
Take heed not to sour God by whitewashing the departed.
Eulogies will not absolve souls on the Day of Judgment.
Confess your *own* sins to cleanse your *own* soul's garment.

Bonginkosi

Broadcasting pound-sterling confetti hid his dark side.
At night he delved in voodoo, the coy effigy cast aside.
Strangely, stray children disappeared near his villa.
I once saw him trailing one and offering her vanilla.
The children, sacrifices, he took to shunned juju gurus.
This he alluded to one night when he had had one too many,
But presented himself as an Abraham sparing his Isaacs;
The sheep had to die for his children of the promise to live.
Interred in a cove were skulls testament to a covenant entered.
It was an altar and as long as it stood the sheep had to die,
A tabernacle demanding slaughter for its annual incense.

I protested but he dared earmark me for the next ambrosia.

Anger and contempt and disdain rose in me and I was filled.

I thank God for His mercy I was neither maimed nor killed.

But my father two years ago was seized by some hysteria.

He daggered himself at his Presidento St Redd Cafeteria.

Disembodied of his faculties he disembowelled himself.

All this before dining afternoon clients and serving staff.

Fr. Flynn
(*Shakes his head and says emphatically*)
So far you have not yet confessed any sin of yours.

Bonginkosi
Pardon the narration, which serves to prepare you, Father.

Anyway, as his right-hand son from his senior wife

I inherited his estate. We feasted on all foods and cinnamon.

Next day a *sangoma* brought a gourd to me at midnight.

It was the sole item in a small reed basket,

But the bearer sweated profusely in that cold night.

He said he was in pursuance of the last will and testament

Of my father; unwritten, unendorsed and mind boggling.

Upon my father's death I had to take custody of the gourd.

My old man was dead and the *sangoma* had a solemn task

To honour a dead man's word; so did and said the bearer.

On my doorstep he left the basket and vanished into
the night.
So with the estate came a bearded, beaded, hairy
gourd.
Souvenir-like, its beadwork was uncommon but
devilish.
Disquieting; on the beaded gourd was a phallic
protuberance.
In defiance of decency it pointed like a hail-Hitler
salute.
This ungodly feature I'll euphemistically call finger.
Its fetish function was disturbingly apparent,
Persuading me to seek ways of discarding it forthwith.
But the gourd is telepathic and reads my mind ahead
of me.
It baffled medicine-men and self-proclaimed prophets
And claimed lives of diviners while growing in
virulence.
I then couriered it by DHL to Pyongyang, in North
Korea
To a pen pal whose religion seemed the *Matsubayashi*
dance
The Korean wound a pink Christmas ribbon around it
And by urgent courier consigned it back to my duplex
Stating in a letter she was Taoist, verily to gifts averse
And to that end had appended an Oriental scriptural
verse:
All things are within Tao; why should we need gifts?

Fr. Flynn
(Mutely expresses bewilderment and impatience)
Get to the point, my son. Your earthly Father must
rest.

Bonginkosi
I doused the gourd with A1 jet-fuel. To no avail.

I sprinkled it with anointed water. Its beard grew
longer.
I deserted it in a commuter omnibus. Only to find it
home.
Logic-defying occurrences took over my new-found
life:
About to fall asleep, I heard your voice saying my
Requiem,
Totemic and wholesome with my Zulu clan name
Khumalo,
Jerking me awake to the tear-jerker of tear-jerkers –
silence.
Food began to run out mysteriously, especially
delicacies.
In the closet the gourd stood in a pool of fresh blood.
Remedy: gulps of vodka, a stupor, then hopeless hope
I was becoming insane, hallucinating or, better still,
dreaming.
Dutch courage gave way to shell-shock: a man came
out,
A swarthy being, knee-tall, wide-eyed, wiry and
grizzled.
Of sacrificial human blood and staggering wealth he
talked.
I collapsed and came to hours later, thanks to my
fiancée
She rang the bell that raised me, maybe from the dead.
Whether it was a man or drink conjured him I know not.
Days later the gourd featured in my fiancée's dreams.
In her nightmares the gourd appeared in its exactitude
Yet I had been totally discreet about its existence.
In that dreamy world it roared its vulgar aptitude
Savaging, molesting, raping and sodomising her.
God pardon me, an inexplicable syndrome overtook
her-

A continuous menstrual flow, house-arresting and
punitive,
Puss-oozing pubic blisters that rendered her
vegetative,
An agonising lock-jaw and ruthless choking followed.
She was in the shadow of death and under its tow.
You might require proof, her grave is in Soweto.

Fr. Flynn

Horrifying, but succinctly accounted, my son.
I perceived a sublime truthfulness in your account.
But a bloody goblin was left in your custody, a *tokoloshe*.
The Blessed Madonna's *Memorare* is your perfect refuge.
I will intercede for you right now, my beloved son.

Both cross themselves and bow their heads.
(Praying)

Come to recall, O most gracious Virgin Mary,
That never was it known anyone who fled to your
protection,
Implored your help or sought your intercession was
left unaided.
Inspired with this confidence I fly to you, O Virgin
of virgins,
My Mother; to you I come, before you I stand, sinful
and sorrowful;
Our Mother of the Word Incarnate, despise not my
petitions,
But in your mercy hear and answer me. Amen.

Bonginkosi

Amen.

Fr. Flynn

Let us not abandon your fiancée until our petitions
Have conducted her soul into the holy abode of our
Lord.
For her death atone with three decades of the rosary.
You shall recite the *Memorare* in the morning and
evening.

Do so indefinitely until you receive a response from
God.

But in her honour betake yourself to a hospice or
orphanage.

Be there one full weekend, your province menial
chores.

Our Blessed Mother is your buoyancy from this
precipice

A donation in humility at the end of the day would
be proper.

May the peace and grace of God our Father be with you.

Bonginkosi

Father, freak accidents are consuming my siblings.

My mother died recently, killed by ants on the lawn
at the villa.

Relations are ever in hearses, dead or accompanying
the dead.

No one can be industrious anymore except to attend
funerals.

Man of God, death and destruction dog us.

My helpless extended family is in a ruckus.

Fingers are beginning to point, a Zulu witch-hunt is
brewing.

It culminates in razing down of property, banishment
or death.

My summit of inheritance, the business empire, is
crumbling.

Captain further this ship I cannot; it is embalmed in
an iceberg,

The Scorpions might soon be out for me for tax-evasion.

A long silence

Fr. Flynn

Son, besides absolution for your sins,

What else were you requesting from our gracious Lord?

Bonginkosi

(*Untying duffel bag*)

You are God's representative in this parish, a man of God.
Duly God vested divine power in you to edify
parishioners.
I came to surrender the gourd for destruction, Father.
Pray I that you destroy it by fire, unction or other
means.

Fr. Flynn

The closing eon is not an era of miraculous supremacy.
My hands are bound; I am a man of flesh and blood.
Honest to God, when cut I bleed blood scarlet.
Jaundiced I would cry for the Lord's healing and mercy.
May this cup pass to some other priest in the diocese.

(*Dismissively*)

Your time with the Lord you have had.

BONGINKOSI *draws a gourd from the bag and rises abruptly.*
It has immaculate beadwork around its neck, cowry shells for eyes
and a life-size phallic projection. He holds it to the confessional
aperture.

Bonginkosi

(*Peering into the priest's booth, incensed*)

Other priests pleaded with me to consult a hermit.
They refused to admit reaching their minds' limit.
With rancour they dismissed me from their presence.
You being the vicar, father to them and us all
To no one but you I must submit the faceless menace.
It's etched in my mind that the Church is my refuge.
God's armoury is at your disposal; smell the incense.
Pause a while, revered anchor, and be meditative.
To whom but the vicar would I surrender this?
Among men you're God's earthly representative
Cuddled in my refuge I refuse to look elsewhere!

FR FLYNN *rises and peers through the aperture too. His eyes bulge*
in horror at the sight of the gourd. He steps back in caution and
slightly stooping, peers at BONGINKOSI'S *face.*

36

Fr. Flynn

Your father did not pursue peace with every man.
Calm down. A victim of your father's greed you are.
Our God punishes up to the third and fourth generation
For the sins of the fathers. By appealing to me, you err.

Bonginkosi

Damn it, Father! My family is ravaged and perishing.
Stranded in a death-trap stand I helpless and cornered.
At this demon's leisure I shall soon be conquered.
I am on the verge of surrender to evil and its devices.
My perception was that this God of war and vengeance,
To Whom for years we bowed to in praise and worship,
Whose power we beheld through good health and riches,
Whose holiness we sang and whose praises chanted daily,
My belief in the resurrection would effortlessly oblige
To rescue me from life's pitfalls and the devil's vices.
Honestly, from life you force me to opt for a withdrawal.
Yet by deduction, beating about the bush, cast aside
All my avowed and pious priest says is: 'Calm down'!
With coercion you haggle with me to consider suicide.
But in this church my conviction and tithes are etched.
With diffidence my devotion you stifle with a dedication
Therefore despite my reverence this is my declaration:
Henceforth, the gourd is now the property of the Cathedral!

Fr. Flynn

(*Pointing at him in admonition*)
     I know who you are;

Bonginkosi, the son of Mathebula, the late extravaganza!

As heir to a tycoon's empire you raised media typhoons.

This is worse than nuclear waste; be gone with your bonanza!

Dump that devil here and I will get you arrested, Bonginkosi!

Bonginkosi

(*Contemptuously*)

Arrested! Arrested at the behest of my priest and father!

What a pathetic excuse for a priest! A disgrace to the Pope!

Fr. Flynn

Yes, my son, I will have you arrested for witchcraft,

For the death of Sindi Ramakutana of Soweto, your fiancée.

The harrowing *Scorpions* will book you for tax-evasion.

My boy, you are deuced if you walk out without the goblin.

Fr Flynn fishes a tape recorder from an inner breast pocket of his jacket and holds it out to the aperture.

You will excuse me for capturing your confession.

Instinctively I record some confessions for such moments.

Both of us can destroy each other today or some day.

Reiterate I; I am a man of flesh and blood, Bonginkosi.

The face of God and His power I have never seen personally.

Moments of anxious silence pass; FR FLYNN *holding out the tape,* BONGINKOSI *the gourd.*

Yes, I am a man of God but also a man of infirmities too.

At times atheistic, at times Gnostic, oftentimes confused.

Your plight requires the services of a sanctioned exorcist.

Bonginkosi

What does it take to bring an exorcist to South Africa?

Fr. Flynn

Prayer, convincing reports and hierarchal interventions.

Bonginkosi

Please expound the procedure, Father Flynn.

Fr. Flynn

(*Sighs*)

Very well, my son. Patience and applications.
I will have to apply to the diocesan Bishop.
Who will apply to the revered Archbishop.
The Archbishop will convene a meeting
Between himself and the African Affairs Cardinal.
The Cardinal will write to a Vatican Committee.
The Committee chairman will notify the Papal Advocate.
The Papal Advocate will then apply to the Pontiff.
The Pontiff will peruse the reports at his leisure.
If satisfied there is a vague evil called *Tokoloshe*,
And a parishioner is terrified and in grave danger,
Papa will assign one of the few Catholic exorcists.
This exorcist might come after several long years.

BONGINKOSI *shakes his head, picks the duffel bag and throws the gourd inside. He sinks on the bench and sighs with exasperation, the bag between his feet, and holds his head.*

Bonginkosi

You win, gladiator-like, very much unlike a priest
The unrepentant sinner in you is enormous.
Now hand over the tape and I will take my leave.
All these years I didn't realise you were so venomous.

Fr. Flynn

(*Smiling shyly*)

Understand a Mexican stand-off, Bongi.

We should be dreading each other like fire and
dynamite,
Like two equally militant superpowers braced for war
That can churn and bombard each other with
blitzkriegs.
Your acquired knowledge of my carnality is a missile.
The tape in my possession can destroy you in a day.
But smile, this day we're mighty Russia and America
Secretly signing a non-aggression and mutualism treaty
May the Almighty God have mercy on both of us,
Forgive us our trespasses and bring us to everlasting life.
Wearily, BONGINKOSI *rises, looks scornfully at the aperture
and walks out of the booth the duffel bag on his back. Exit*
BONGINKOSI. FR FLYNN *sighs in relief and kneels in prayer.*

Curtain

SCENE THREE

Sunday evening
A spacious bedroom in the vicarage of the Roman Catholic Cathedral of Christ the King

There are two closed inner doors in one of the walls; one is to the toilet, the other to the hallway. The windows have chintz curtains. The bedroom's brickwork, fittings and architecture are that of the Cathedral. Among the room's refurbished Victorian-style furniture are a grandiose double bed neatly covered with a duvet, a chest of drawers, a bureau with an open Holy Bible on it, a cushioned, exquisite settee with a small coffee table before it. On the table is a wireless radio playing low Catholic choral music. The chest of drawers is shrine-like, laden with a paraphernalia of Catholic items; figurines of Madonna and the Child, crucifixes of Christ of various sizes, etc, etc. Framed portraits of the current Pope and his predecessor are on the walls.

Still in his previous attire, the suit and priest's collar, FR FLYNN is crestfallen and ponderously motionless in one of the chairs, the only movement being in his right hand working the beads of a rosary. The chair is in the centre of the room.

Fr. Flynn

(*Soliloquising*)

Should I heed the subpoena and lose face at the Vatican?

Should I don a visor, brace myself and go...

To that throbbing heart of rheumatic Roman Catholicism,

To that pneumatic cocoon of severity of indoctrination,

To those paedophilic ninjas in red togas and scarlet skullcaps,

To those somnambulistic Juggernauts in fiery apparel,

To those expressionless Draculas somnolent as cud
cows?
Should I knowingly surrender myself...
For these accursed vultures to pleasure themselves
By having a field day to toss and down-dress an
Irishman?
Should a created man submit to other created men?
I am an Irishman, a descendant of heroes, not a
fledgling.
I sinned against God and not judgment-thirsty
Cardinals.
Had I octopus tentacles I would suck them dead
Jiu-jitsu them to death in that disciplinary chamber.
With Ninjutsu jab them with their power and
authority.
Beware, empty-handed the ninja prances with ease,
But behold, a thousand and one weapons are his.

He pauses and shakes his head

Get out of me, Satan! Submit myself to them I will.
Sheepishly I must heed the call to the slaughterhouse.
This self-abdicating arraignment before self I must
end.
Like a squadron I must will my unwilling self to battle.
Hitherto I have died many times before the execution
From the wheals of self-scourging and condemnation.
This detonation of self is not the way of a matador
With decency and courtesy I must accept my exit.
Why should I disrobe a thousand times before the
day?
If Christ submitted to his torturers who am I to demur?

He shrugs and sighs.

I could throw in the towel but surely live the life I
fancy;
I have enough tape recording to blackmail enough
moguls

And raise enough wealth to live in Hollywood
flamboyancy.

*He crosses himself reflexively, rises and heads towards the en-suite
toilet door, undoing his collar. Exit* FR FLYNN *into the toilet but
leaves the door ajar. Moments pass. The noise of splashing water
occasionally rises above the choral music.*

Enter NAOMI *tentatively from the hallway and closes the door
behind her. She is in a provocative, figure-hugging mini-skirt and
blouse, but expensive and immaculate. She looks around the room
appraisingly and, without looking, flings her handbag on the bed.
She goes to the chest of drawers and picks up some of the figurines,
which she kisses and sets back. She saunters around looking at wall
decorations and the portraits like a visitor to an art gallery. At the
bureau she casually flips some pages of the Bible but resumes her
tour. Then, with her back to the door, she bends and begins to remove
her high-heeled stiletto shoes. The sound of a toilet cistern flushing
reaches her, but she continues to remove her shoes. Moments pass.*

Enter FR FLYNN, *barefoot, from the toilet and, startled, stops in
the doorway baffled by her intrusion. He is in underclothes; a white
vest and shorts. His suit and shirt are draped on his forearm. The
same hand is carrying his shoes. He freezes a pace inside the bedroom
and looks at her, at the handbag on the bed, and back at her bent
figure.* NAOMI *removes one shoe and turns to the other.*

Fr. Flynn
(Sternly)

I demand to know your business in my quarters, lass!
For God's sake no one will understand you intruded.
This is my private bedroom, not the confessional!
And this manner of dress provokes the end of the
eon!
You reckon it isn't a quarter to the accursed
Armageddon?

Naomi
(Pulling off her shoe without looking at him)

For the sake of decency

Should I have visited tied up in grave-clothes?
Neither in flesh nor in clothing is the essence.
Were you going to stand my sight in a head-cloth
Like grave-clothes-covered Lazarus risen from death?
I came to confess; to right my crooked ways with God.
To that end I present myself before you a man of oath.
In the synagogue our Lord conquered the opposition.
Let us please God and not reason and stifle the spirit.

Fr. Flynn

(Holding up a hand to forestall protest)

Frankly you seem a fusion of a wreck and a freak.
Naomi, we must do the good thing –the right thing.
You walk a weird wayward alleyway like a maverick.

Naomi

But people who do good do not go to Heaven, Father.
It is those that do not do well, but believe, who inherit;
Those that do not care if it's a synagogue or a
bedroom.

Fr. Flynn

(Stepping back)

Hmmm! I had underestimated your lethal venom.
You somersault perilously between life and death.
By your tongue you jeopardise yourself and cast
snares.
Your banal words are a physical assault on my
eardrums.
It is the devil's tendency to draw others into the
doldrums.

Naomi

(Straightens and turns to face him. In mock plight)

Then pray for me, purge me of the evil you perceive.
Father Bryn Flynn, I know you have a mind to sieve.
To receive salvation came I earnestly; not to deceive

He continues to stare at her. She strides to the settee and sinks on its edge, her posture and bearing erotic. She begins to cross and uncross her legs, fidgeting, finally lowering FR FLYNN'S *gaze to them.*

Fr. Flynn

This is absurd, Naomi, kindly confess and go.
I can see you are shameless mortal sin incarnate;
A clear festering and obnoxious suppurating evil.
I won't mortify myself with an obscenity like you
Sinfully disposed with wiles of gangrenous seduction.
No matter how you extol yourself, I can perceive
That you are a demon risen from the deepest sea,
A complete antithesis of the ideal Catholic child.

Naomi

I found a tramp in the confessional booth and fled.
Punctiliously I present myself to be rid of my sins.
And this is the royal welcome for a parishioner!
The Schweppes-and-schnapps fraternal reception!
That bespeaks stewardship and the decreed compassion!
In demonology, how do you parley a seeming apparition?
Is it by riveting your eyes on the slender legs of a child?
Is it by lending yourself to the fear of an alleged devil?
Is it by flitting into an en-suite toilet for refuge?

(Smiles)

Madonna and the Holy Child are they art?
Golgotha ordained you with fortification to withstand.
If Calvary the foundation was a hoax the hour has come.
Humankind must turn away from this venerated fallacy
For ages thought to have founded the venal galaxy.
Tonight light and darkness make rendezvous,
The planets, you'll see, will glacially flounder.

Fr. Flynn

You sound and seem on an apocalyptic mission.
What was bidden in the beginning cannot be reversed.

Time was of the essence and the brutality was
incensing
But Christ prodded Judas to betray him without delay.
Diabolist, I order you to do quickly what you came to do.

NAOMI *laughs coyly, briefly, and rises from the settee.*

Naomi

Sauntering suggestively across the room like a model,
almost unmindful of his presence in the doorway.
Is the essence of a spikenard fragrance in the air;
Prompting you to deduce dangerously like Judas
Iscariot?
Employing a mind wearied by law and statutes,
Pontius
Thought logically to recuse himself and dodge to err.
Whenever you stop and reason, against God you riot.
To God, Alpha and Omega averse to reckoning, point us.

(*Looking at a large crucifix on the wall, her back to him*)

Athena emerged full-formed from the forehead of
Zeus.
Greek mythology can as well be my newfound
religion.
Poseidon, Apollo, Hephaestus and all the other gods
I could bow to on condition I am not labelled a fiend.
Well, Naomi and the priest are now caged in a
bedroom!
What do you reckon will come of this encounter?

FR FLYNN *shrugs and crosses to the chair at the bureau. He
drapes all his clothes on its backrest and talks as he puts on his
clothes, the pair of trousers first.*

Fr. Flynn

Why come provocatively dressed like this?
I sniff a scandal in the making, but at your age
I read you like unadorned Stone Age calligraphy.
Capture the created image and its offence:
The timing, the scene and the pornography
Of a priest in his underclothes set to retire,

Alone with a schoolgirl in nightclub attire,
It's late at night and the two are in his bedroom.
We're like two lovers in a dacha on a lonely shore
Surely someone desires to see me pulling a rickshaw.

FR FLYNN, *now donning his shirt, sits on the chair and shakes his head in bafflement and shrugs to himself while looking at NAOMI'S back. She turns from the crucifix and quickly walks to him. Stooping slightly, she peers in his eyes without blinking, their faces inches away from each other.* FR FLYNN *stares back into her eyes but is unsettled and attempts to rise. But she makes a face, puts a hand on his shoulder and presses him down. His mouth opens but she puts a finger across his lips.*

Naomi

I came to talk, Father, after that take I my leave.
Let this be an impromptu reformatory for a delinquent.
A solemn responsibility you have to reshape a dastard.
So willingly I came to be remoulded to standard.
In the course of it should I turn seductive understand
My intent it wouldn't be, but an incursive will
That overtakes my faculties like high-grade mustard.
Should that moment come, Father, remain calm.
A man of God appointed by God is always at the helm.
You will order the head-rearing devil to return to Hell.
Hurry, Father Flynn, in the morning comes dew.
For now redemption, my sole concern, is overdue.

FR FLYNN *considers for a while. She removes her finger from his lips, smiles warmly at him and saunters to the chest of drawers.*

Fr. Flynn

(*Buttoning his shirt*)

It appears your definition of redemption is to confront.
Neither now nor in the future will I connive against my piety.
If I violate my vow then against myself I become an affront

Unworthy of myself and the Shepardship of God's
parish.
God above, if I so much as touch this vulture with
my hands,
I declare that without rites of sepulture to my body I
must die.
On the spur of that moment despatch Michael with a
sword.

Naomi

Ask me, perversity comes like a thief at night.
Everymen is vacillating, inconsistent and unstable.
Be warned of the risk of swearing thus, inviting
tragedy.
Recant your words, Father; of the archangel Michael
Only ruthlessness, brimstone and devastation are
written.

NAOMI *rises and strides to the shrine-like chest of drawers. She
picks the figurines and begins to toy with them, then deliberately
drops one on the floor, startling* FR FLYNN *as it shatters.*

O God, how thrifty of you to make us live only once
But generous of you to grant us the destructive ability
To destroy others and ourselves without recourse.
The life of a human being is like a sparrow's flight
Through the bright lounge of a majestic palace
From eternal darkness into brightness and warmth.
Poor sparrow flies in through one door and exits the
other.
He would want to perch but this is not his residence
He must make the most out of that brief flight in the
light.
Then forever vanish into the wintry archaic darkness
again.
Book One transpired in the incense-filled Cathedral.
Now, fired up, in essence we are set to start the sequel.
Have you ever had the experience of sexual
intercourse?

Fr. Flynn
(*Astounded*)
>No. Oh yes; in my adolescence, of course.
Naomi
(*Pointing at him with the figurine of Maria*)
>Priestly life is solitary; obviously you desire marriage.
Fr. Flynn
>Is marriage an ordained stipulated carriage
>To whisk a chosen creed to some New Jerusalem?
>The blessed miracle and mystery of Salem
>With neither parentage nor lineage,
>Nor origin, relations or age,
>Walked this earth a king and a ministering priest
>Chaste he was and God's friend paid him homage.
>Grasp this and you will be like the wise men from the East.

FR FLYNN, *now fully clothed, fastens the priest's collar.* NAOMI *smiles and picks another figurine.*

Naomi
>An octogenarian but agile Germany aficionado of mine,
>A shipbuilder and tobacco merchant living in Durban
>Dauntingly tempts me with a handsome payment
>For a tattooing of his Aryan names and trademark
>On my fragile Easter eggs and the whorls of my girlhood.
>Says he can go further to build me a small Hall of Fame.
>What is your advice, Father? Is it a blessing or a shame?
Fr. Flynn
>You have opted out of conventional living, Naomi.
>At your age you let geriatric eyes peer at your girlhood!
>You have become a taboo-free specimen from Troy.
>I would hazard and suppose your future lay in sainthood.

49

You render restless your mother's soul with your audacity.
But why do you digress when you have come to destroy?

Naomi

I can subdue pain better than a yoga guru;
It's not that I am weighing to tattoo or not to tattoo.
Neither am I in pursuit of lectures on what is taboo.
My body bears all sorts of them; dragons and serpents;
Permanent reminders of the dominance of men of means.
In business and on feminine bodies they desire monopoly.
Everything must be a billboard advertising their empires.
Well, it isn't by choice that I know these things, Father.
From the soft purrs of these perverts I derive my fees.
To remain on the pedestal I ought to be a lewd da Vinci.

Fr. Flynn

(*Rises abruptly with finality*)
Your talk is nothing save high-sounding frivolity.
Judging by your temerity and your youthfulness,
You are a well-read young girl, Naomi, but a falsity,
Beguiled by a studious mind steeped in reptilian bile,
Meticulously guiding yourself to your own destruction.
A demented scorpion stings itself to death in its vile.
On your tongue are words upon words;
Words void,
Words Manichean,
Words waffling the arrogance of a sham liberty
Words that seek to foreshadow the Second Coming.

NAOMI *laughs and doubles over, touching her knees. Still laughing, she staggers to the bed and sprawls prone on it for a while. Now suddenly silent, she props herself seductively on an elbow and looks at him, which seems to unnerve* FR FLYNN. *From her handbag she draws a pair of scissors, arranges pillows against the headboard and coyly lies on her back on them, the scissors on her chest.*

Naomi

(*To the ceiling*)

Father, this is the honest truth now.
For gathering the sheep a stewardship crown awaits you.
With great craftsmanship you preach, the sheep appreciate.
But when you stand behind the altar in your flowing robes,
Your cathedral voice lifted to God's abode in the Heavens
And you bless the Eucharist, the chalice held high,
I have always fallen in love with you in spite of myself.
The piety you exude and your gaiety, both torturous
Coupled with the lit romantic candles, churn me into jelly.
For you only I break my maniac love for the prosperous.

Fr. Flynn

Child, that is the attraction of the blessed Eucharist.
It is euphoric and comes from above to edify the spirit.
Your satanic interpretation of anointing must cease.
Because of this pull many women have defiled priests.
In the things that please us, God we continually displease.

Naomi

(*To the ceiling*)

Do not deny me my manna, Father.
Be a good father, Bryn. I promise to be a good child.
What manner of a father are you who doesn't give?
Perhaps you might benefit from a discourse:
In the supra-mundane of giving and receiving

The giver upholds neither the gift nor the recipient
In his blessed giving the giver gives outside self.
The crucifixion is an exemplar par excellence to this.
The Lamb was not ignorant of this concept of giving
Hence on behalf of harlots and all sinners He tasted
death.

Fr. Flynn

(*Stamping his feet*)

Come hellfire or hailstorm, to evil I won't concede.
Keep the name of my Lord out of this madness.
I could enjoy your delicate Dresden-china beauty
Not to have and to hold, but the sight of it,
Like a father admiring in earnest a daughter's beauty.
Notwithstanding the way you present yourself
Cleave me; chide me right, left and centre
The wild orchid garden I will not enter.
To me you will always remain a child.
Show me not the cloven hoof further, leave now!
Be gone, little devil, or it takes throwing you out!

Naomi

(*Calm and still speaking to the ceiling*)

Oh, your voice becomes succulent when you shout.
God is not going to reward a bovine Irishman.
Catch-22 this might be for you if you want it to be:
Indulge and accord a schoolgirl her fantasy.

Fr. Flynn

But I would displease and anger my God.

Naomi

In the Cathedral you are Caesar, sultan and sheikh.
As ruler accept my homage in flesh and cease to shake.
Keep your distance and I will rent my clothes and
shriek.
You would rot in Johannesburg's correctional grime
Among aberrational misfits raised on dope and crime.
Stalwart Soweto cut-throats committed to thwarting
society

Will cleanse you of your self-destructive piety.
And you will be born-again from Christianity.

Fr. Flynn

We must talk, Naomi. You threaten my reputation.
This repulsive game of yours must cease forthwith!

She sits up suddenly, grabbing the pair of scissors and holding it against her side, a free hand unbuttoning her blouse. Her countenance is fiery.

Naomi

This isn't a ceremonious cannon volleying blanks.
My scream can reach every corner of Johannesburg.
I stand on a dais calling the shots and here there are:
Take off those damn clothes and for once be romantic!
At an over-spilling dam you stand, yet you thirst.

(*Viciously*)

This is the last time I instruct you, Flynn!

FR FLYNN *gingerly begins to remove the suit, jacket first, down to his underclothes. He drapes the items on the backrest of the chair again. He stands forlornly near the chair avoiding her gaze.*

This place has the aura of the shrine at Lourdes.
Take down the popes before they steal the mood.

FR FLYNN *crosses to the wall and takes down the portraits of the popes and other Catholic decorations and places them face down on the floor. As he does so* NAOMI *removes her blouse and casts it away.*

(*Arms outstretched, the pair of scissors in her right hand*):

Now come, matador, tonight we shame celibacy.
Come to mamma for entertainment, my occultic white ox.
With self-restraint you poison your conscience needlessly.
Come for the attainment of the summits of lunar mountains.
Suffer no misgivings, this life we live only once.
On Judgment Day plead coaxial confusion and coercion.

53

FR FLYNN *starts towards her, but suddenly from off-stage the boom of police and fire engine sirens and bells reaches them. The noise rises to a crescendo.* FR FLYNN *freezes. There is frantic rapping on the quarter's main door off-stage.*

Off-Stage Voice

(*Panicky*)
>Fire!...Father Flynn! Fire! Fire! Fire! Fire!
>The Cathedral is on fire! The church is burning!

(*Pause*)
>Father Flynn! Flynn! Father Flynn, are you in?
>He-eey! Fire! The Cathedral is on fire! Father Flynn!
>Fire!

FR FLYNN *and* NAOMI *glance at the inner hallway door and stare at each other. Moments pass. The sirens draw nearer and nearer as* FR FLYNN *gingerly climbs onto the bed and sits forlornly besides* NAOMI.

Naomi

(*Beckoning with both arms*)
>Let the Cathedral go up in plumes to Heaven!
>Burn it must for the Kingdom has its reasons.
>There immortality, prolonged boredom, awaits it.
>Let the sacrificial asphalt lamb burn, burn, burn.
>At God's disposal are legions for all seasons;
>Some to gather together, some to scatter, some to assault,
>Some to make altogether, some to unmake mankind.
>Blasphemy supposes angels require human reinforcement.
>Logic stifles the soul, opposes the spirit and suppresses it.
>If the Roman Catholic Cathedral of Christ the King must burn,
>This urban monument of auburn stone and fire-crafted panels,
>This gilded Tsarist crown proudly projecting into the sky,

If its stained glass must crack and crumble, its
pinnacles melt,
If its Madonna and the Holy Child portraits must fall
and shatter,
Irish boy, only God above, the Comptroller, would
have willed it.
In his Holy of Holies He will ecstatically sniff the
plumes.

NAOMI places his hand on her stomach before drawing FR
FLYNN *over her. Smoke begins to swirl into the bedroom. The
church bell begins to clang in panicky, quick succession. The off-stage
door is banged frantically again. The sirens are suddenly loudest and
are killed one after the other.*

Curtain

Act Two

THREE MONTHS LATER...

SCENE ONE

Evening
Inside a cabbalist's prayer chamber, Jerusalem

The décor; stars of David and Yiddish-inscribed banners and prayer shawls cover the walls. Candles in clusters of seven are burning on stands and on the floor. Striking about the arrangement is the symmetry of the candles, i.e. half of the room is like a reflection of the other. RABBI Ben AVUYAH is seated cross-legged centrally on a cushion with his back to the wall. A prayer shawl is draped across his shoulders. Two old tomes are before him within arm's reach. BONGINKOSI is sitting on a cushion, too, to the Rabbi's right, but his knees are propped up. The duffel bag is at his side. The Rabbi is looking at the tomes and at Bonginkosi intently in mystical contemplation.

Rabbi Avuyah
Stranger, welcome to Israel, the Promised Land.
The born-again compromised to God's disdain.
Sojourner, this is the holy Canaan, a journey's end.
Distance yourself from falsehoods and wisdom attain.
In the natural, marvel at the Church of Nativity.
Be agonised when you stand on the hills of Golgotha;
To the Roman, execution was an act of creativity.
In awe stand in the empty tomb and lose your self,
That is how the Gentile who lands here burdens himself.
This is the land of the Torah, scriptural alpha and omega.
Cabbala from the sages of blessed memory is pure divinity
For the Sinai plains, valleys and tracks tortured the flesh.

In the Talmud are milestones for the latter-day
sojourner.
Many seas have treacherously changed into the Red
Sea.
Again welcome to Israel, away from Pharaoh's Egypt
Feast your eyes without ceasing; day and night sightsee
But beware the fallacy of logic and archaeology.
This is the holy fatherland of rabbis and avowed
Pharisee
Ordained to remove the blinkers from the
uncircumcised eye,
Who, as prophesised, perilously harp their eulogy.

(Gestures at the two tomes)

The Jerusalem Talmud or the Babylonian Talmud?

BONGINKOSI *gingerly points at the tome near him.*

The Gentile selects Babylonian over Palestinian sages.
As *Adonai* formed the firmaments Cabbala was born
And the Exodus was laid out from Egypt to Canaan.
In every generation every man should set forth,
Must set forth and is en route from one Egypt to
another.
Shaddai guide you to open a page and point a passage.

BONGINKOSI *leans forward, opens the tome near him and points
to an area. He straightens and sits silently in awe.*

Life is a river.

(Looking at the passage and reading):

From the Babylonian Talmud
Our Rabbis taught: Four entered an orchard[Apendix 1]
And these are they: Ben Azzai and Ben Zoma
Aher and Rabbi Akiva. Rabbi Akiva warned them.
Against falsehood warned Rabbi Akiva:
Do not call water pure marble
Nor call pure marble water.
Ben Azzai gazed and died.
Ben Zoma gazed and was stricken.

Aher cut down some shoots.
But Rabbi Akiva departed in peace.
Moments of silence prevail with BONGINKOSI *looking bewildered. But* RABBI AVUYAH'S *eyes are riveted on the text.*

Bonginkosi
I do not understand, assist me, Rabbi Avuyah.
(*Gesturing bafflement*)
Life a river?
(*Thoughtfully*)
Ben Zoma?…Rabbi Akiva?

Rabbi Avuyah
The text read I to you again, Gentile.
Upon encountering cataracts and boulders
A river does not complain nor cease to flow.
To bear its load to the high seas are its orders
Nothing hinders it, neither man nor heavenly claw
(*Reads slowly pausing between phrases to look at him*):
From the Babylonian Talmud
Our Rabbis taught: Four entered an orchard
And these are they: Ben Azzai and Ben Zoma
Aher and Rabbi Akiva. Rabbi Akiva warned them.
Against falsehood warned Rabbi Akiva:
Do not call water pure marble
Nor call pure marble water.
Ben Azzai gazed and died.
Ben Zoma gazed and was stricken.
Aher cut down some shoots.
But Rabbi Akiva departed in peace.

Bonginkosi
Still it remains veiled and elusive, Rabbi Avuya
I perceive the meaning like some drifting aroma.
Like the scent of sepal-swamped fruit of cocoa
(*Shakes his head*)
Ben Azzai… Ben Zoma?
Kindly expound and satisfy my curiosity.
The brevity is to the mind an adversity.

61

Rabbi Avuyah

On three journeys you embarked.
Life being nothing but a river,
Out you went to three seers of repute.
If I err here and now kindly refute.
The first you undertook to Ben Azzai,
Against what confronts you seeking an assegai.
The second you embarked on to Ben Zoma,
Founder of aromatic honey who partook and died.
The third journey as shoot-cutter Aher who lived.
In short, on this journey of no short-cuts and dispute
This is your fourth as Rabbi Akiva to Rabbi Akiva.

Bonginkosi

(*Scratches his head and strokes his chin*)
You bewilder me further, Rabbi Avuyah.

Rabbi Avuyah

Your selected text points at three journeys undertaken.
On them embarked you as a corpse, pall bearer and
undertaker.
Three journeys you undertook as foolish Nicodemus.
He elected to bow to Baal's panoramic manifestation
Abrahamic wisdom ingrained in him was forfeited in
one night.
Tell me about your journeys, or you might think the
text lies.

Bonginkosi

Six months ago, acting on advice, I travelled
To the border town of Beit Bridge in Zimbabwe.
Along I took my sordid acquisition and inheritance.
At nightfall I went to a *Johane Masowe* shrine in the
hills.
At the reeds, crosses and earthen vessels I marvelled.
There knelt I before the Prophet *Madzibaba*
Chrysogonus.
There went I after being convinced by others of his
prowess,

That he had the ability to harness powers of light and
darkness;
Was an interface between divine light and apocalyptic
shadow.
There stood he in white robes, larger than life, his
loins girded.
The patriarch Abraham he called in word and long
drawn song
And Joshua, then with mantras Michael was to earth
guided.
All called he into a saucer-like earthen vessel with a
pebble.
The séance and the set-up were overwhelmingly pious.
My duffel bag I placed before him and retreated a
little.
I watched expecting a scuffle both physical and
spiritual.
Chanting known and unknown angelic names and
deities,
Like a priest in the Holy of Holies before the revered
Ark,
The prophet sprinkled my bag with water from the
vessel.
He untied it, gazed inside, clutched his chest and
tumbled.
The prophet's eyes rolled; he died of an acute heart
attack.

Rabbi Avuyah

(*Looking at the text*)
Of Ben Azzai it is written:
Ben Azzai gazed and died.
Of him it is elucidated:
'He that speaketh falsehood shall not be established
Before mine eyes.'
Prove the Talmud wrong.
Narrate your second journey into the wilderness.

Bonginkosi

To an Islamic Sufi mystic I was directed
Into far-flung Cape Town I visited a Palestinian
Moslem.
He greeted me by name and took me into his Sufi
chamber.
Spread he the Quran before him and chanted the
names of Allah.
He gazed inside my bag, rent his clothes and ran amok
naked.
To this day he is demented, says a very reliable source.

Rabbi Avuyah

(*Looking at the text*)

Of Ben Zoma it is written:
Ben Zoma gazed and was stricken with madness.
Of him it is elucidated:
'Hath thou found honey?
Eat as much as is sufficient for thee
Lest thou be filled therewith and vomit it'
Prove the Talmud wrong.
Narrate your third journey into the wilderness.

Bonginkosi

I journeyed to Nigeria, to a place in Oyo near Ibadan.
Led I was to a Yoruba village in awe of a renowned
egúngún.
To the village *Oba* I presented ¥sÍ òkè, palm oil and
cola.
Gladly he pointed to an evergreen forest, his sanction
manifest.
With a guide trekked I endlessly under gloomy
canopies,
Our weapons a blunt machete and the guide's ancestral
songs.
After eternity the forest broke into a bald, shrub-
dotted plain.

Mounted sombre ensigns of human skulls flanked the
footpath.
In that plain stood an age-old sagging *iroko*-tree, its
aura *òrò*.
Under it ambled a juljul-ringing, ochre-smeared juju
guru.
The *aróso's* voice was hoarse from calling *Orunmila*.
In his presence sat I and also presented him with cola.
Because I was a foreigner he took off his wooden
mask
And I cringed at the sight of cicatrix marks on his
face.

Rabbi Avuyah

On lighter things you dwell to your detriment.
You talk like a clown, like one not in a predicament.
The medicine-man bellowed: *Orunmila! Orunmila!*
Omni linguist Yoruba divinity of facts and divination!
From the jars around him he drew and offered you
cola.
For the gourd he called out twice: Ikwela! Ikwela!
From the underbrush emerged a skinny heat-reeking
bitch.
Chanting mantra after mantra he held the dog by the
collar.
Thrice he struck the gourd with the tail of a hyena.
Forthwith fell silent the cello-like orchestra of insects.
With a hand steeped in palm oil he uncorked the gourd
And stuffed it with *iyan*, ground cassava and paprika.
Into the opening poured he goat milk, rice wine and
vodka.
The gourd jiggled and shook, vibrated and hopped.
Its protuberance moved up and down like a pharynx.
When it perspired he smeared it with the dung of
hyrax.
Before your eyes the bitch and the sweating gourd
mate.

In Oyo and Ibadan townsmen wore goggles and looked up.
As the man explained that the evil was worse than an *àbikú*
An unpredicted total solar eclipse was darkening the day.

Bonginkosi

Rabbi, my pickle is an ordeal apocalyptic
Nothing is hidden to your favoured eyes.
I am obliged to say your divination is cinematic.
Before the act was over he raised a scimitar
Like an executioner's sword it beheaded the bitch.
Above, the sun inched out of its lunar concealment.
Below, the weird sudden darkness almost bitumen-pitch
Steadily gave way to light under the silenced firmament.
The medicine-man filled the gourd with the dog's blood.
With another scything sweep of the scimitar,
Surgically-precise, amid whistling and mantras
Like one with a gift for précis, a *babalawo* killing *ebon*,
The recluse severed the phallic protuberance in half.
For now, said he, Yoruba gods had halved the problem.
But solemnly placing the fallen half in a small basket,
The juju guru ordered me in a voice funereal to buy a casket,
Of an infant; a small wooden affair with obituary flowers.
This, stressed he, to bury the fallen half at midnight
And avert consequences because the blood-gushing piece
Was the fragment of an infant's soul that had to rest in peace.

Rabbi Avuyah

Move on to the burial and the prolonged graveyard eulogy

Of an innocent child kidnapped and slaughtered as *ebon*
Whose grave was a cairn with no epitaph, no date nor name.
But you returned to civilisation; your hotel room in Ibadan.
Alone laboured you with the rosary pondering things bidden.

Bonginkosi

I had to find wads of the pounds, dollars and euros,
High denominations thereof, to fill the casket to the brim.
As bidden I did, but after flying back to liquidate the empire.
At night we trekked to an old graveyard, under the gaze of owls.
I carried the money-laden casket, a baby weirdly crying inside it.
The medicine-man as undertaker we laid to rest the fallen half.

Rabbi Avuyah

Move on to the send-off, Gentile, the eulogy forego.
The gleam in your eyes rouses amusement when you speak.
On a hanging cliff you stand dicing with death and vertigo.
Unaware you're in the shadow of death and a speck
Yet unwisely you dwell on a bitch spotted with vetiligo.

Bonginkosi

Said the Yoruba medicine-man at the graveside:
For now as thunderous *Shango* casts shadows on you
And his blinding lightening darkens darkness
Fear no more, for you are no longer marooned
But stand akimbo on a boulder at the riverside.
Fear not the *òrò* cult's bull-roar and the river's roar.

The *oogun* of Yoruba gods has broken the siege.
Your head high you will hold and walk in peace.
Unharmed you will walk though evil hums your dirge.
As the ballad of owls and vultures flies into your ears
In *Orisa-nla*-gilted peace you will walk in godly peace,
For *Ogun* has gathered enough spearheads to protect you.
After crossing the viciousness of death-roaring rivers,
When you rest under birch-trees and shady *iroko*
In their boughs will be distressed lianas and mambas.
At night when Sindi's tremulous voice calls your name,
Your fiancée's footsteps shall approach your doorstep.
Beware of reproaching a demon in footstep form,
Its modus operandi piety, grit and attraction of pity.
Be wary of knocking and the soft calling of your
name.
Answer at your own peril the infant's calls on Death's
back.
As you walk in the night of your inherited darkness,
Death determinedly awaits the lowering of your guard,
For the infant to cry no more, and Death to look
elsewhere.
But for the complete eradication of the quandary
Albino blood was required, so prescribed the juju
master.

Rabbi Avuyah

(*Looking at the text*)
Of Aher it is written:
Aher cut down the shoots.
Of him it is not elucidated
When the Yoruba man cut down the manhood,
The virulence of your acquisition was halved.

Bonginkosi

Rabbi, lack I the heart to sacrifice an albino.
Came I to you for a solution righteous
Before God, man and angels. 'No'

Is my pennant held high for angels to know
That at heart I am not murderous.
Murder would my heart ceaselessly gnaw.
My reward to you shall be generous.
Mystical power and compassion you embody,
Prescribe some animal, even a rhinoceros
Whose blood I could rub onto my body.
Succumbed you haven't unlike Chrysogonus.

Rabbi Avuyah

Cabbala does not advocate the slaughter of albinos,
Or any animal . Nor does it delve in goblins.
Of Rabbi Akiva it is written:
Rabbi Akiva departed in peace.
Of him it is not elucidated for he did not look.
But falsehood Akiva did not speak. Gaze, he gazed not.
Die, he died not, neither was he stricken with
madness.
A family man I am, and a leader of a synagogue.
This is your fourth mystical journey.
The mother of mysteries is that you are Rabbi Akiva
And he that you consult is Rabbi Akiva.
Journey on; the Exodus did not end at Mara.

RABBI Ben AVUYAH *hastily closes the Talmud and removes the
shawl from his shoulders.*

Pity you I can, but help you I cannot;
The diadem of grace is not upon your head.
Paganism is a noose around your throat.
Never have you striven to mediate on the Torah
Nor to seek the Lord God of Israel since you were
born.
Of ascent into Heaven you dream with morbid
certainty.
But from the rock from which you were hewn
Never have you reflected in deed and in words.
Because of your entrenched belief in the trinity,

You are blasphemous to God by appearance.
Glean the Aramaic books with understanding and
reverence.
Thus divine sages of blessed memory hinted:
That the Gentiles are not idolaters but Jews in
carcasses
Yet their lives are rooted in idolatry.
Satanic ways to acquire wealth point you to perdition.
The wealth and the tools are wreaths of generational
curses.

Bonginkosi

Rabbi, what must I do to lead a normal life again?
All my wealth I buried in a graveyard in Nigeria.
My father was propelled by faceless evil and gain.

Rabbi Avuyah

Your father was in league with the Devil.
Rich he already was when he bought the fetish.
Had he lived his days in contentment –
Performing good deeds in discernment,
Being a father to the fatherless, husband to the widow,
Marrying off orphaned boys and girls,
Consoling mourners and memorising psalms,
Adonai would have kept him away from the evil
charm.
Few men more wicked than your father walked this
earth.
Adolf Hitler, a demon from Hades, brought the
holocaust
But unlike your father he didn't will nor cause his
family
From distant relations to his nearest and dearest at
any cost
To inherit death and perish like slaughterhouse
animals.

Bonginkosi

It was his sinfulness, not mine. For the slaughter of Abel

Should Cain's son be guillotined? Tell me, Rabbi.

If so, then in the eyes of the Lord I am a rebel.

Rabbi Avuyah

The Torah cannot shine on the face of the uncircumcised.

Your redemption is hidden in the Apocrypha.

As it was prophesied and written,

Because your father's blood is in your veins

Yours is a remorseless exile in the desert.

For now sing the words of the Hagiographer

Until synagogue doors are flung open to the Gentiles.

RABBI Ben AVUYAH *quickly rises.*

If I exit before you, something will tear you down.

Take heed, sojourner, and insist at your own peril.

The countdown started before the firmaments

The dictates of the inner man are your filaments.

When you see an owl, do not say: 'Owl, Owl!'

Call it a dove because it is one in this realm of likeness.

Remember light was born out of created darkness.

Journey on as bidden. You might as well sightsee.

A river's flow does not end on merging with the sea.

The thud of extraordinarily heavy, slow footsteps approaches from off-stage. Both look in the direction and BONGINKOSI *discerns the sight of something frightful. Eyes bulging, he rises in terror, while* RABBI AVUYAH *languidly raises an arresting hand at the approaching enigma out of sight. The heavy thud of footsteps stops.*

This is Hayyim, a golem, hero of a dormitory in Auschwitz

From dust he was raised by rabbinical chants august.

When called upon he brought calamity to the SS sentry.

From Michael's stable, he is deathless like a ghost

This is the slaughterer summoned to Egypt at Passover.

At your own peril stay, Gentile, and continue to stare aghast.

RABBI AVUYAH *lowers his hand and the thuds resume their slow approach.*

BONGINKOSI *flings the duffle bag on his back and bolts. Exit* BONGINKOSI.

Curtain

SCENE TWO

Daybreak
Inside Naomi's flat lounge in Johannesburg

As the curtain opens darkness is waning; natural light is coming in through the windows. The corpse of the Police Commissioner of South Africa lies face-down in the room; stout, white and over fifty years old. The body is in a long-sleeved shirt and undershorts. The shirt is ripped in several bloodied places. The bloody corpse lies at the foot of a couch, the blade of a large kitchen knife embedded to the hilt between the shoulders. Blood is everywhere on the floor, in pools and blotches. A service pistol lies near the body. Folded neatly on a chair in the centre of the lounge is the South African police uniform with a stately, decorated service cap on top of the attire. Polished shoes are under the chair. On a coffee table are a half-full wine bottle and two glasses still holding wine and a banquet of roses. A stereo is quietly playing the South African National Anthem^{Apendix II}.

Enter NAOMI, in a revealing frilled nightdress, from an inner door. The dress is bloodied. She is drunken and drinking in gulps from a wine bottle. Here and there singing along with the stereo and staggering mildly, she paces the lounge, seemingly oblivious of the body. Finally she switches off the stereo and looks down at the body.

Naomi

(*To the corpse*)

The National Anthem, always a prelude to a hanging
Not a befitting tribute to the man who called the shots
But all the same a token thereof in good faith for a hero.
Once resplendent in a bemedalled uniform, now zero.
How the mighty has fallen! Forlorn like a lunar rock!
At the coast of Normandy the Last Trumpet bade farewell

Its tonality an appeasement and tear-drawing long wail
To the thousands who fell breaking the Atlantic Wall.
But it only sounded for some seconds, at most a minute.
Yet for you I played the National Anthem for hours on end
As though you were some statesman beyond reproach
Worthy of your calling and more colourful epaulettes.
The time and energy I expended in honouring a cockroach!
Officer, I should be torn with grief and shaking with the fear
Of what is to come, but in all honesty I feel empty.
Any tale of a lizard and a panda has a sad denouement
It's neither the corpse nor the blood that disturbs me
But death's ability to denounce life and enter unannounced.

(Soliloquizing as she drinks and paces)

Bedevilled by mishaps these past three months now I know
That absent in me are genes and chromosomes of prosperity.
Johannesburg's thousand cultures and bewildering diversity
Infused and assimilated in this slaughterhouse called city
Is a cold-hearted maniac-making treadmill unstoppable.
This is the epitome of a devil's devil of every sin capable.
O jaundiced incinerator! Thou art a constipated alligator!
Mutton, pork and beef you churn out, not as an abattoir!
But people as mooing cattle you masticate and gulp
And out comes villainous swine as the quartered meat;

Least of them speakers of language foul, which is
the offal.
Inhabitants you welcome hopefully, young and old
And being bearer of the accursed archetype to mould,
You sculpt your citizens into everything God is
against.
Sodom and Gomorrah would envy your wickedness.
Demented I could be becoming, walking on the blood
Of a dead Police Commissioner, the pride of the
President.
This man, described as a luminary of order was a
dissident.
Against South Africa and God he warred day and night
Because upon his appointment he swore to uphold
the law.

*Wobbling, she stops and looks down again at the body and glares
furiously at it as she speaks.*

My heartfelt condolences to your wife, a rose soon to
wither.
My delayed felicitations on your married life void of joy.
If it had happiness in it you wouldn't have been my
prey.
May the powers that be forever spare her the
heartache, I pray
Of not knowing his last words or what devoured her
husband.
The gun-carriage he has missed and songs from the
Brass Band
May she never see his remains or know what
transpired.
O without full military honours its hard to believe
you expired.
Now I have no integrity, the Devil has forfeited my
soul.
Defeating and frustrating justice is now my objective
sole.

If I leave room for failure surely I will face the
executioner.
What has Jo'burg grilled me into, Police
Commissioner?
I am now less honourable than a flea in heaped
compost.
Have I not become a humbug and odorous street
lamp-post
For the convenience of peripatetic dogs with loose
bladders?
This roulette! This pursuit of pleasure gives me
shudders.
See how societal decadence and values suffering a
dearth
Can conspire to belittle a man and ultimately cause
his death.
But what do I do with you, worthy Sir? Consign you
to maggots?
Survival instincts evade me when I need them, like
gold nuggets.
But cover you I must, to shield myself from your
brazenness.

Exit NAOMI, *staggering through an inner door. Re-enter* NAOMI
*presently, carrying a linen bed sheet, with which she covers the body.
From the chair she takes the service cap and places it on the corpse,
stately-like. She steps back and appraises the covered, still form,
then crosses to the couch and sinks onto it.*

One charm of my splendid character is non-hypocrisy.
Naturally in my daily existence without any bidding I
fabricate.
In my ramblings I bless the names of gods but also
fornicate.
Habitually, if there's enough time on my hands I
masturbate.
To check the hallowedness of a place of worship I
desecrate.

I am jealous but I am not timid and bear no lengthy
grudges.
But despite all this I am as extraordinary as the River
Ganges.
I refuse to be ordinary, to be a termite among termites;
A myopic owl among owls, an ordinary girl among
girls.
For years reading and conformity have failed to
contain me.
If anything, studying the malicious dictators of the
world,
Hitler and the sundry Hitlers now manifest on the
continents,
Shows that it is of greater benefit to suppress others
than to be pious.
If historians learnt from history, billionaires would
abound.
What good is it to research and teach what you won't
accept?
If a credulous fool were to hear me they would think
me evil.
I bear not the 666; I am a schoolgirl with a genius for
absurdity;
Adventuresome and profane, these being my
profundity
My nagging thoughts 24/7 are bestial and
pornographic.
No one but me would interest the National
Geographic.

For a while she sits in contemplative silence. Her thoughts are projected
by a ventriloquial voice resembling hers, i.e. her lips do not move in
the projection of her thoughts.

Ventriloquial Voice

(*As Naomi sits in silence*)
A man's character is segmented like a millipede,

But the segments separated from the others like sausages.

Knowledge of man is myopic acquaintance with one segment.

Some segments are stately, courteous and ceremonious.

Others are saintly and papal in religious adherence.

Yet others exude a Hitler-like warmongering belligerence.

South Africa knew a stately anti-crime Comm. Smut

But the Commissioner of my knowledge was a cave-dweller,

An onanist maddened by my pulchritude and youthfulness.

I was the Hagar-punctuation to the sad sentences of his marriage;

The pervasive colons, commas, exclamations and indentations

That diligently divided his day from night, service from sleep.

I was his anaesthesia against the heartache of childlessness.

With paragraphs of erotica I formatted his cheerless pages.

We were as different as the bee and the flower; hence the draw.

But in his mind I was a flower the way biologists know flowers;

Some days he made me pleasure myself for his enjoyment.

The caveman never came to his doll empty-handed or crestfallen.

Aware a schoolgirl ate more than a rabbit and was insatiable,

He filled my purse with rand and dollars, my handbag
with kits,
My flat with opulence, and my mind with police top-
secrets.
Despite all his efforts I couldn't conceive passion for
him.
Love is a profound enslavement utterly
incomprehensible.
To pronounce it is admission to total compromise in
all things.
Only those prepared to overlook terrible human
weaknesses
Can fall in love and flourish hand in hand with their
dear ones.
It's a bottomless pit that devours millipedes with
voracity.
People propelled by adventure fall in love out of
curiosity.
The desire to demystify a person's character is the
motive.
Instead of frankly saying: 'Ma'am, allow me to
discover you'.
They borrow hackneyed phrases from ancient
wordsmiths
And dress like Star Trek actors so to appear
combative,
Then await an opportune moment only to say: 'I love
you'.
Lovers, indeed explorers, seek to sate an insatiable
spirit
Of discovery like that of a thirsty bullfrog on the
brink
Gloating and drooling at a Hyacinth-covered still
pond.
Surely for a frog, a satiating providential gigantic drink.

A self- enthused leap. Plop! Agitating widening ripples.
The palm-size green islets choreograph a samba dance
Down he goes, heart-pounding like a gold stamp mill,
Into the depths conspicuously iridescent with goldfish.
But starring piranhas and hungry jellyfish roam for a meal.
Cyanide and nooses often bring the rear of an epic love affair.

The ventriloquist's voice stops as NAOMI *speaks in person;
continuing.*

Naomi

Telling him he had filled my womb turned him wolverine.
Last night I waited for the mood to become romantic,
Then I told him what the kit had told me, that I was pregnant.
Abort, insisted the Commissioner. Abort! Abort! Abort!
The old fox must have known already; he took out pills
And ordered me to take them immediately. I protested;
The Pope and the Government and God are anti-abortion.
A scuffle ensued that took both of us into the kitchenette.
There he talked of statutory rape, his job and blackmail.
This the panda did, holding a service pistol to my temple.
But the lizard was quick. Lashed I at him with the knife.
Maria jammed the pistol for the sake of the unborn child.
Now perforce I must think. I must put my brains to work.

Rid myself of the body I must or I will face the noose.
She gulps the wine in silence, thoughtfully, then continues.

I should have discarded the body and the uniform
last night.

But shock petrified me; the horror of the gore I had
created.

*Jumps up suddenly and begins to pace, her thoughts heard from the
ventriloquist*

Ventriloquial Voice

(*As* NAOMI *paces the room*)

Comm. Smut was an amoeba, a discreet master of
disguise.

Always he left his car blocks away and dressed like a
woman.

Always at midnight, always alone, always amusingly
predicable.

In drag came he, but in tunic favoured he to act his
fantasies.

Now here he lies, stabbed like Caesar. I have turned
Devil!

You turned Devil! And killed him like a beast of the
chase!

You lashed at him with athleticism. By your hand he
fell.

But it had to be some devil from the depths of Hell,
Naomi;

To cut a man like lamb chops, and seek to disembowel
him!

O! I had turned Devil! O! I had turned Devil. I am
the Devil!

Hello, Devil. Hi, Devil. What's up in Johannesburg,
Devil?

Perchance you must think, you fool, you bloody
enchantress,

This body is evidence of a murder committed, think,
think.

Think, remorseless vampire; conjure a plan, murderess.

A pause in her thoughts and the voice comes again.

I bemoan your absence, Fr Flynn… gone… gone… gone.

Surely, Comm. Smut needs requiem, my soul, confession.

Gone three months now, poor boy. No hope of seeing you.

I suffer nostalgia of games better than the Olympics.

Sad, sad, sad, babe. The young and the dead. Could be a title.

For a book. A movie. A TV series. I could be dreaming.

A long nightmare. Wish it were a nightmare. The blood,

The smell of it. It isn't, Naomi. Can't be. This is too drawn.

Too elaborate. It was night. Now day is breaking. Morning.

Of course, I can't attend school today. This is nightmarish.

If dreaming, you ought to be falling and falling, your custom.

So this is what it means to kill? But to be dead is something.

But I don't feel as if I did anything. I don't feel like Cain.

O! Was Cain the slayer supposed to feel remorse and pain?

Maybe I was too tipsy. Maybe it's somewhere in my head.

I could be a demon. Yes, I'm a demon. The Cathedral burned.

Firemen, policemen and parishioners converged in no time.

It was real and remains so because we were caught
red-handed.
Poor boy, Flynn, could only stutter before nuns asking
Why we were locked up when the Cathedral was
burning.
It was the Cathedral that burned not some sod or
fallow.
Cops had to take us for questioning. Flynn needed a
burrow.

*Ventriloquist's voice rises to a shrilling tempo. NAOMI freezes, her
face contorts, and she brings her free hand up in a drunken attempt
to cover her head*

Murderess… Murderess… Remorseless murderess!
No! You put it contemptuously as if I wasn't
compelled!
With his last breath he christened you Murderess!

*Silence. NAOMI sighs, shrugs several times and resumes pacing.
The voice becomes gentle but persuasive.*

You're too young to make the headlines for murder:

Voice comes in mock news-reporting formality

SCHOOLGIRL STABS COMM SMUT…
COMM SMUT SHREDDED BY GIRLFRIEND…
COMM SMUT BUTCHERED BY
SCHOOLGIRL…
Under the banner headlines they will place the
evidence:
A large colourful photo of your lounge…*my lounge*…
Showing it is as though a bull was slaughtered.
And there, insert in a corner, Naomi's portrait.

Voice mimics cable news reporter:

The Commissioner of the South African Police,
Comm. Smut, was found stabbed in a flat in
Johannesburg,
In a pool of his own blood, in unclear circumstances.
The late Commissioner was a man against the franchise
That gave criminals, especially drug barons, power…..

Voice becomes hers again, but speaks promptly, staccato-like.
>   The body. Chainsaw. Where to hire a chainsaw?

The revving sound of a chainsaw in action fills the room momentary and stops.

>   Will cut and slice and shred the man to pieces of pieces.
>   Cuts of cuts, slices of slices and shreds of shreds.
>   Then pack him in travelling bags. Or piecemeal in a handbag
>   And take him round the city, dishing him out to stray dogs
>   For them to enjoy like horse meat and boerewors.
>   Or throw him into the Rosherville Dam at night. Period.
>   Sorry, no state funeral for you in the Transvaal.
>   Strictly no casket. You come out in my handbag. Yes.
>   No eulogising. No banquets. No wreath. No hearse.
>   But the chainsaw isn't ideal. Can't hire and operate it.
>   No. I will cut him to pieces with knives and choppers,
>   Burn everything of his and mop the place with acid.
>   With acid? Yes, if I can find it. The place will be clean.
>   Naomi

(Takes over from ventriloquist)

>   I must cut you up and discard you before you turn rancid.
>   I must garner courage or invite some devil into me
>   Or from the sight of his inside I would like a cat mew.
>   I wouldn't want to shock visitors or myself when I sober.
>   Let me get on with the job or some bastard might call.
>   O! He spoke his last words, disjointed though, in Boer.
>   They came out feebly, piecemeal; perhaps a prayer.
>   But on the verge of death, when sight was deserting him,

When he was ashen and had ceased to be a blood-
sprinkler,
And, like a fountain gurgling and choking on his own
blood,
His knees buckling, he appealed for mercy with his
eyes.
Though he must have cursed me, I felt pity for him;
This man now succumbing to death was not my
attacker.
Perhaps it's the segments. Perhaps he was possessed.
I must get the tools now to chop and cut him to pieces.

NAOMI *sets the bottle on the table. The ventriloquial voice begins
to recite the Catholic Memorare as* NAOMI *goes about in silence.*

Ventriloquial Voice

(*Sorrowfully reciting the Memorare*)

Come to recall, O most gracious and dearest Virgin
Mary,
That never was it known anyone who fled to your
protection,
Implored your help or sought your intercession was
left unaided.
Inspired with this confidence I fly to you, O Virgin
of virgins,
My Mother, before you I stand, sinful and sorrowful;
Our Mother of the Word Incarnate, despise not my
petitions,
But in your mercy hear and answer me. Amen.

Exit NAOMI *through a door leading into the kitchen. Shortly she
comes out with four kitchen knives, one serrated, and a chopper. She
puts them near the body and exits into her bedroom. Re-enter* NAOMI
*from the bedroom with two large and empty travelling bags. She
places them on the floor near the body too and looks at it
sorrowfully. She stoops to remove the linen but quickly straightens on
hearing the mounting sirens of police cars. Fear transfixes her. Within
moments the sirens are ear-splitting loud and fall silent. A firm
masculine off-stage voice speaks through a loudspeaker.*

Loudspeaker

THIS IS THE METROPOLITAN POLICE!
I REPEAT. THIS IS THE METROPOLITAN
POLICE!
THIS APARTMENT BLOCK IS SURROUNDED!
COME OUT WITH YOUR HANDS IN THE AIR!

NAOMI *hesitantly crosses to a window and peers out through the curtains, looking down. Bringing her hands to her chest and shaking her head in self-pity, she leans on the wall and sinks to the floor.*

Naomi

(Breaks down crying, squatting against the wall)

The trigger-happy vultures have cordoned off the area.
All those brutes with guns! O! Virgin Mary, where art thou?
Hurry Michael to my rescue, outside people scurry.
O! How did they ever know? How did they ever know?
They will fry me on the chair or hang me like a pennant.
I am not a murderess, but how do I convince them?

Loudspeaker

EVERYONE STAY INDOORS!
REMAIN CALM AND NO ONE WILL BE HURT!
WE KNOW YOU ARE IN THERE WITH HIM!
YOU KNOW THE MAN HAS HEART
PROBLEMS!
DO NOT COMPLICATE YOUR LIFE, MADAM!

Naomi

(Rises; has regained some composure. Crossing to the couch)

No, I won't let anyone enjoy the pleasure of killing me.
My life, mine democratically to live, I am taking right here.
My life, mine democratically to waste, I waste right now,
But at bay I must hold them to buy time for absolution.
Pray fervently I must to St Clare, Patron Saint of poor souls.

Smoother my last thoughts, I pray to the Virgin Mother.
But from where do I garner the courage to take this
life?
Do I solicit it from God or pry it from the hands of
the Devil?
Dead I will drop. O! Madonna, but in whose stead
am I?

NAOMI *drags the couch and places it against the door as the
loudspeaker voice comes again. Gingerly, she crosses to the body and
picks a pointed knife.*

Why do we worry about death when we can self
conquer?
Who does the world applaud: he who conquers
himself?
Or a mighty warrior who fought in many battles now
conquered?
A thousand men I have conquered, now self is
conquered.
O! Sharpest knife, cast I agony from your long blade.
An eye for an eye is the foolishness of our forebears.
O! Hari-kari, wise exit ever impromptu, my flesh I
mortify
This hideous moment is the last frame of years of
reels.
O! God above, my sins of commission, You alone
can rectify.

As the loudspeaker comes again NAOMI *kneels beside the body,
crosses herself and brings the tip of the knife to her navel, holding
the hilt with both hands. She begins to breathe heaving her shoulders
and looks up prayerfully as her arms shake vehemently.*

Loudspeaker

THE BLOOD INDICATES HE IS INJURED!
YOU CAN'T HAVE DONE ANYTHING WORSE!
DO NOT LET THE SITUATION GET WORSE!
AN AMBULANCE IS WAITING, MRS NDLOVU!

Naomi

(*Perplexed*)

Mrs Ndlovu?

Loudspeaker

THIS IS YOUR HUSBAND, MADAM!
DOMESTIC DISPUTES ARE SOLVED
AMICABLY!
COME OUT, YOUR HANDS RAISED, MRS
NDLOVU!
GROUNDFLOUR APARTMENT NUMBER TWO!
YOU CANNOT CONTINUE TO HOLD HIM
HOSTAGE!
EVERYONE STAY INDOORS AND NO ONE IS
HURT!
COME OUT, MRS NDLOVU, WE APPEAL TO
YOU!
REMEMBER ME FROM DAYS PAST –SGT
NXONGO?
WE'RE AWARE OF YOUR SCHIZOPHRENIA!

Naomi

(*Relieved, she casts away the knife and sits on her heels*)

O! The prayer to the Virgin Mary worked wonders.

Thank God there are after the ever-fighting Ndlovus.

NAOMI *quickly rises and returns to the window.*

(*Peering out*)

Aha, there emerge the restless Ndlovus,

Obese *MaNdlovu* holding a knife to her husband's neck.

Poor Ndlovu is drenched in blood, but at least he is alive.

Of course, he is perilously hurt, he needs the ambulance.

But as much as he needs to be whisked to a casualty ward

Sergeant Nxongo would do with an urgent refresher course.

O! jostling Johannesburg, alabaster city of false
alarms!
But occupation with relief sits ill with the task at hand.
Turning from the window, she quickly crosses to the body and takes
both its ankles in her hands.
The bath tub is ideal to deal with a dead officer
So the tub be it, Comm. Smut, honourable Sir.
NAOMI, *with much difficulty and strain, haltingly drags the body*
away as the curtain closes.

Curtain

SCENE THREE

Midday
Inside an august chamber in the Vatican, Rome

As the curtain opens to a people-free chamber, a bell toils at spaced intervals and a high-noted soprano diffuses into the room. Six chairs in a row are behind a longitudinal counter. Perpendicular to the counter, near its extremes, two judicial witness stands face each other; one for the plaintiff, the other the defendant's dock. Microphones can be seen on the stands.

Enter six white Roman Cardinals in single file, hands clasped reverently and all uniformly dressed in red skullcaps, predominantly red and white robes. CARDINAL DUCCIO PIETRO di NICCOLO, dressed as the others, brings up the rear. He is carrying a thin leather folder. He goes to stand in the plaintiff's stand. The six CARDINALS sit behind the barrister counter.

Enter FR BRYN FLYNN a moment later, from the opposite side, in immaculate parish robes, escorted by two ceremonial Vatican guards in medieval battle attire and bearing long spears. FR FLYNN steps into the defendant's dock as the two guards retreat two paces in unison and stand at attention. FR FLYNN and CARDINAL PIETRO face each other across an empty floor. The bell falls silent.

Card Pietro
(*Addressing Fr Flynn imperially*)
> I, Cardinal Duccio Pietro di Niccolo, of the Roman Curia
> On behalf of this Jury of Cardinals sanctioned by the Pontiff
> To be the Pontifical Committee for Discipline
> In the case of Father Bryn Flynn from South Africa
> Hereby, without bias, prejudice or favour,
> Deliver the Committee's verdict as agreed and as follows:

He opens the folder and reads.

On the count of an improper relationship with one
Naomi.
(*Looks up*)
The Committee finds Fr Bryn Flynn guilty.
On the count of arson that almost destroyed the
Cathedral
(*Looks up*)
The Committee finds Fr Bryn Flynn guilty.
On the count of coercing Zanele Tshabalala to abort
(*Looks up*)
The Committee finds Fr Bryn Flynn guilty.
On the count of Zanele Tshabalala's culpable murder
(*Looks up*)
The Committee finds Fr Bryn Flynn guilty.
On the count of breaking his oath of celibacy
innumerable times
(*Looks up*)
The Committee finds Fr Bryn Flynn guilty.

A long pause. FR FLYNN *gazes indifferently at* CARDINAL
PIETRO.

Like our Lord who was granted leave for His
mitigation,
Before the Committee, as per procedure, may pass
sentence,
Fr Bryn Flynn, you have free scope to air your
mitigation.

Cardinal Pietro sits.

Fr. Flynn

Cardinals and you, Governor from the Roman Curia,
I am neither a Roman apologist, nor am I a Nazi
sympathizer.
But suffer I an impasse; interchange I Pope with Fuhrer.
Look out the window, there, stands *Collegio Militare*,
A lugubrious monument to a genocidal Nazi rampage,
Vigorous *prima facie* evidence of a relationship
improper!

A thousand souls commandeered right under papa's
windows,
Yet in his opulent apartment crapulous Papa protested
not;
The scurrilous no-contest that made a thousand
widows.
Brutal irony reigns supreme in this Vatican chamber.
A bloodied beast arraigns a poor priest for cleansing!
O Psalms! Lo! Thou art, by the hands of men,
relegated!
O Vatican Law! Thou art, by the hands of men,
elevated!

(Shows his palms)

To wash stains from a man's palms
Baptise him in a raging river of blood stilled with
depth!
Though here and now I stand in the belly of the beast,
Having pleaded no-contest before man as before
sworn,
Cardinals and you Governor, my combat sword is
drawn.
I maintain my innocence before man, only against God
I sinned.
I am deluded; I do not know what my business is
before you.
That, in outline, is my mitigation statement to the
Committee.

Card Pietro

(Outraged)

Father Flynn, like a deranged haranguer
You harass our sensibilities. Aghast we are
At your vitriol, digression and your accusations
This is not The UN Assembly, the Rome Statute or
the ICC.
This is an august Committee appointed by the Holy
See.

Fr. Flynn

I did not come to be applauded by neo-Nazis in skullcaps.

Card Pietro

(*Voice grating*)

Do you plead scathing accusations, innuendo
And unfounded parochialisms of history as your mitigation?

Fr. Flynn

The laundry and the launders are dirtier than the linen.
But as per your demand I reiterate my position for the record;
Nota bene, not as mitigation, but to benefit procedure.
In my head of arguments said I this, Your Eminences,
The weights had been diabolically placed on the balance;
On one side metric tonnes, on the other seemingly an ounce
Thus the dilemma of dilemmas was horned:
A compound of loss of sheep, repute and imprisonment;
Weighted against the breaking of a vow of celibacy.
I, Flynn Bryn; flesh and bones, a man, not the papacy,
Stood crucified on the pivot sweating drops of blood.
But with me did not stand still the hands of time.
Of Christ it was liturgically expressed to the Romans of old:
The Son of Man was crucified; into Hell he descended.
There, inside the Devil's tempestuous citadel, prevailed He
For the glorious iridescence and justification of humankind.
In essence, take note of sequence, verily He had to descend.

Card Pietro

Defendant, astoundingly you militate against your defence.
Be guided in my wisdom; an impromptu sermon is no mitigation.
Like Bacchus you ejaculate, wasting great opportunity.

Fr. Flynn

The gist of it you miss, Cardinal Pietro di Niccolo,
Not only you, but the entire College of Cardinals.
The Lamb treasured nothing, thus wrought He salvation.
Caught between a celibacy vow and his beloved flock,
A good shepherd breaks the vow into a shepherd's crook.
I, being no Laodicean, from our Lord took a cue.
But, alas! Instead of a papal award, you hold out a sarcophagus.
O! This hearing is nothing but a body-viewing queue
Your furled, whorled, flowery robes, the funeral banquets.

Card Pietro

If that is your mitigation, assuredly it is entered as presented.

Fr. Flynn

It hasn't rested; how then can it be entered, Cardinal?
Or upon contest, the sentence shall be declared void.
Well, let it be put on record that you tire of hearing me.
But hastily add I this to this blameless Committee:
In the comfort of your splendid cedar-panelled chambers,
While biting Havana cigars and sipping dry red wine,
Lousily you busy yourselves with dockets and dockets,
Diabolically issuing set verdicts like a ship's pennants.

Many men have fallen pell-mell because of your
myopia.
Where I minister I deal with treacherous demons,
With promiscuous wives in matrimonial distress,
With bloodthirsty, prayer-defiant goblins that waste
lives.
But unlike you I am not an addendum to the
adornment
Of St Peter's sacred tomb with my apparels and
person.

Card Pietro

(*Shakes his head mildly*)

Are you still in possession of your faculties, Father
Flynn?

Fr. Flynn

(*Nods energetically and adds pitch to his voice*)

As a living memorandum come I; not as a coward,
To bring your focus to issues pertinent, issues
devouring.
In Africa the Devil is not something you read in the
Bible
He has sundry forms that lure and bedevil ruthlessly.
It is atrocious for you to dilly-dally in petty accusations
While willy-nilly the Devourer wolves the sheep.
I see you are Pampers-swathed pupae in demonology,
Still illogically dialogising whether Adam had a navel,
Or between Good Friday and Easter Sunday,
bracketed within,
Are arithmetic three days and nights, while the flock
suffers.

Card Flynn

(*Perturbed, says sarcastically*)

This is the hearing of Father Bryn Flynn,
Defending himself in chief on allegations of
immorality,

That allegedly culminated in the death of one Zanele
Tshabalala and the loss of the life of an unborn child.
Overwhelming evidence was presented against the
defendant.
Father Bryn Flynn, I remind you fraternally, defend
yourself.

Fr. Flynn

Remind I you, Cardinal Pietro, that you are a Sicilian,
A man of flesh and blood, a man of fallibility… a man.
But the infallible Master of the Day of Judgement,
God,
Is not a man that He can turn against His scrolled
Word.
In my fallibility as a man only to God alone plead I
guilty
And am found guilty on Judgment Day, if adjudged
guilty.
Forgiveness is preached loudest from St Peter's
Balcony
But least practised by the entire College of Cardinals.
Cardinals, be guided earnestly, you sit here as solemn
jurors
As if I were the perpetrator of the Holocaust and its
horrors
Because when I sought forgiveness you gave me a
subpoena.
You delude yourselves; the case is not founded on
immorality.
The case is not about Bryn Flynn, an Irishman in
Johannesburg.
This case is about demons, goblins, ghouls and
ghommids
Let loose among the miserable African flock by the
Devil.
Demons come to the cathedral clothed as men and
women.

97

Of the Eucharist they partake and indecently harass
congregants.
Gregarious fetishes and goblins are brought to the
confessional.
I am talking about the spirits of bewitched human
beings,
That Providence or the Devil sends to me daily to
subdue.
But the manuals are silent on fetishes and exorcism
And, Your Eminences, the subduing of *tokoloshes*.

Card Pietro

Gosh! What is a *tokoloshe*?
This gibbering of gibberish,
This yawing yapping and yammering
Of things egregious and things gregarious,
Of things nefarious and things devoid of foundation
This erudition of sarcasm never admissible
Henceforth ends. And end now it does, Father Flynn.

Fr. Flynn

(*Henceforth gestures freely and dramatically*)
My presentation is still in embryo
Yet you disturb me like a yoyo.

(*Gesturing ceremoniously like a courtier*)
You Caesars,
You insatiable Vatican Caesars,
You six Caesars in contemplative silence,
Hold me not in contempt in your reticence
For cease I now my indignation to you by application
For leave to present a *tokoloshe* as counter-evidence.

Card Pietro

Like a weirdo you delve in things unknown and bizarre.
Like a vertiginous vulture you dive and rise in
widening spirals.
At this juncture the presentation of counter-evidence
Is counter-procedure; therefore application dismissed.

A long silence.

I am persuaded to believe the defendant rests his mitigation
Now comes the retreat from whence the sentence.
I, Cardinal Duccio Pietro di Niccolo, of the Roman Curia,
Without bias, prejudice or favour…

Fr. Flynn

(*Interjects*)
This your ceremonious swearing-
(*Parodying disdainfully*)
Without bias, without prejudice and without favour
Ominous Scripture in its righteousness overrides it.
FR FLYNN *steps out of the dock and kneels facing* CARDINAL PIETRO, *his head between his knees. One after the other the* CARDINALS *rise in astonishment.*
Duccio Pietro di Niccolo, is Rome without stones?
O blameless Pietro! Solemnly I pray,
Be the first to stone your prey.

Card Pietro

Rise, Father Flynn, this instant!
Or the Committee in contempt holds you!
(*Furiously*)
The Jurors retreat and the hearing adjourns!
Exit the six CARDINALS *in single file, mildly gesturing bafflement,* CARDINAL PIETRO *leading. The bell toils again as before. The two guards step forward in unison, but* FR FLYNN *remains kneeling. The bell stops ringing. Moments pass. The bell toils again as the* CARDINALS *re-enter and take positions as before.* CARDINAL PIETRO *bears a wax-sealed scroll. The bell stops ringing.* FR FLYNN *is stock-still in his prayer posture. The two guards retreat systematically and stand at attention just as before.* CARDINAL PIETRO *addresses* FR FLYNN *gravely.*
Father Bryn Flynn! Father Bryn Flynn!
FR FLYNN *sits on his haunches and clasps his hands in humility.*
As mandatory, the Pontifical Committee retreated
After having learned your mitigation. The Cardinals

Sitting as jurors, in their avowed unanimity sentence you.
I, Cardinal Pietro, here now deliver the sentence.
(Pauses)
Defrocking! The Committee defrocks Fr Bryn Flynn!
Ritually, the six CARDINALS *rise and bow their heads in unison.*
CARDINAL PIETRO *volleys the sealed scroll across the chamber*
towards FR FLYNN'S *dock but it falls midway. Instantly, the bell*
tolls at a faster tempo and is louder than before, then falls silent.
All the Cardinals cross themselves thrice. The six in the jury box sit.
The Committee grant you leave to appeal.

Fr. Flynn
This did I already, Cardinal, to God Almighty.
In your wisdom, to whom now do I now appeal?

Card Pietro
To God again, Mr Flynn, to the revered Holy See.
Wishfully appeal within thirty days, this being day one.
In the unmaking of a priest God's Representative on Earth
Always has something to say, usually a farewell prayer.
It is now left of me to ask you to stand down, Mr Flynn.

FR FLYNN *rises, smiling sardonically to the astonishment of the*
Committee.

Fr. Flynn
Dracula, I tender my intention to appeal.

Card Pietro
(Firmly)
Stand down, Mr Flynn!

Fr. Flynn
(Pointing at CARDINAL PIETRO *and gesturing wildly)*
Cardinal Duccio Pietro, what unanimity do you pronounce?
You scaly viper from a basket of tempestuous vipers!
For years this Vatican have I frequently visited;
Overtly as a devout priest, covertly as an alligator.
On several occasions I have kissed the Pontiff's hand

And found favour with the most powerful Vatican faction.

Under this mausoleum are vaults, strictly for a chosen few.

Into them crawled I, the alligator, from unlimited access gained.

In my custody are dossiers about your dark sides, Cardinals.

Now at anytime like a desert storm I can raise vicious whorls.

I am not here to bargain for my priesthood, be guided duly.

Card Pietro

(*Raising his hands to silence him with finality*)

This hearing is no longer in session! *Shuttapu*, demon!

Uneasiness registers among Cardinals.

Fr. Flynn

Of malicious arson on my own Cathedral you accuse me

And sentence me aggressively, having retreated only a while.

Yet of specific bank accounts in Zurich, Amsterdam and London

I have developed irrefutable evidence backed by your fingerprints.

I know the Church's dirty deeds and your dealings with drug-lords.

I know about your horrendous orgies in Honduras and Hungary.

And about your paedophilic Olympics in Thailand and Honolulu.

A long and tense silence ensures. FR FLYNN *points at the scroll.*

That scroll you cast at me as if to swine is my visa to the Pope.

Brood of Mafiosi, if I step forward and pick it, mark my words

101

I will destroy your honour and certitude in exactly
three minutes!

*All the Cardinals look at each other suspiciously and fearfully, some
rising.*

Card Pietro

(Like one awakening to reality)
O! *Diabolosi*! Thou art come to destroy Jerusalem?

Fr. Flynn

Draw daggers and kill me in this chamber or
elsewhere,
But rest assured, descendants of Brutus, that a nuance
of news
Or rumours of my assassination or disappearance,
Is the awaited brutal signal for my Cardinals in the
wings
To press the button that unleashes the dossiers on
the Internet.

*The few sitting cardinals jut to their feet as a stronger wave of panic
sweeps across the panel, punctuated by coughs and hushed, quick,
consultative mumblings and restrained gesturing.*

Cardinals, and you, His Eminence Cardinal Pietro
leading,
Verily, do you grant me leave to pick my dismissal
scroll?

*All the Cardinals almost freeze; some mouths agape, some looking
away, some heads bowed etc, etc. Time stands still. CARDINAL
PIETRO involuntarily scratches his temple. Hand outstretched
theatrically, FR FLYNN starts towards the scroll triggering an
undignified noisy scuffle among the Cardinals; as two furious
Cardinals attempt to leave their positions to intercept FR FLYNN.
At the scroll FR FLYNN pauses and gestures bewilderment at the
melee as the curtain comes down.*

Curtain

Act Three

SEVEN YEARS LATER…

SCENE ONE

Daybreak
An open-air Xhosa *sangoma's* rainmaking shrine,
Eastern Cape

It is a small clearing in a rocky dry veldt in a forest. Many earthen vessels of various sizes, some intact, some broken, are disorderly arranged around an ancestral grave. The grave is a simple affair of a mound of rocks. A large horned animal skull on a waist-high pole stands as a tombstone. Various animal skulls mounted on poles and rocks mark the periphery of the shrine. Sunlight increases with the cries of birds.

Enter a lacklustre, unkempt and barefoot NAOMI *in an unfashionable old dress torn in places. A string of beads is around her ankle. She is carrying a large traditional broom. Yawning, she begins to sweep the shrine lazily, her thoughts projected ventriloquially.*

Naomi's V. Voice

(As Naomi goes about sweeping)

    I reckoned as material girls reckon;
    Of ice-cream, pounds, liras and bacon.
    But to devouring depths ghouls beckoned.
    How could I have been aware of the pursuit of sorrows
    That scatter like a hail of cluster bombs, yet are arrows?
    Is it that I was ill-starred from birth or that fate prey-seeks?
    The dark myopic blanket lifts now several years too late.
    How could I have stopped the night that ate me?
    An inkling of thought from a moment of ponder
    Ought to have warned me to raise my arms in surrender.
    In their wisdom the minstrel elders in hoary voices taught:

Waylaying is a promiscuous life for eggs, oats and salads.
In the errors of these philosophers indeed lurked wisdom.
For gold nuggets were dammed in that vast field of dross.
The painstaking irony in it! The threat of blanketing doom!
Decadence had maddened the skyrocketing albatross.
Uncelebrated, I have become like an ulcerous wound.
If the philosophical tutors had plainly spelt life algebra,
Or had clearly stated that coiled in the fresco lotus,
Or loose in the Venetian château of everyone's admiration
Roamed a black widow deadlier than an Egyptian cobra,
I wouldn't have paled to more than a facsimile of myself.

The ventriloquial voice stops. NAOMI *squats and arranges some pots on the grave, rises, and begins to sweep again.*

Naomi

O! This onerous asphyxiating culmination!
O! This ominous nauseating abomination!
To whom do I ascribe its root, to Heaven or Hades,
To a nameless bug in Jo'burg or my mother, Thobeka?
With hanging hidden jowls that rare jewel adorned me;
An erotic investment for the captivity of a soul-mate,
So uttered she, hinting this was the favoured oil anointing.
O! Looking back, that howling winter, I remember
She took me to a very shrivelled old lady, winds yowling.
Thobeka said this was Gogo God-sent to remould the young.

Like a hermit she lived at the edge of a threatening forest.
Cry did I, afraid I had been brought in for decorative tattooing.
But with words soothing mom promised me a trip to Budapest.
My mother placed me in Gogo's custody and callous hands.
For two vainglorious weeks my vineyard Gogo invaded.
On my loins she cast caster oil as she chanted to Xhosa gods.
Like an automan she laboured though to what glory I wonder.
Gogo said she was milking evil out of my bewitched body,
Mumbling: In man's world facades and toys sit well together;
If pleasant to the eye and the finger no divorce clouds gather.
At the end of the ordeal when I looked at myself in the mirror
O Xhosa craftsmanship! To my utter amazement and horror,
The head of an age-weary cock stared boldly back at me.
Was it my youth and pulchritude that made the men drool?
Or it was the weft of this welting goose-pimpled cock
That whetted and riveted perverts to wetting themselves?
To whom do I apportion blame, to gods or to man?
Can I lay it on my mother for delivering me to Gogo?
O in that hut of poles and mortar, red ochre and indigo
An innocent child's attention was brought down.

Do I blame parental connivance that would my youth forgo?

Perhaps Gogo in the fog of senility called the wrong god.

Perchance in her groping she drew oil from an *Itola's* gourd.

Now I war within and without against stroppy Xhosa ghouls.

Could the culprit be this custom that prematurely ages girls?

May be I must lump the blame, and doubly so, on Ngquku

My dad, the gluttonous cock that sold its soul to the Devil;

A barter that saw him surrender his wits in exchange for lust.

Mother out on an errand he stooped low and demanded to see.

Was it my dad or was my dad a tool by some devilish proxy?

In his advances and retreats he thought he was foxy.

It became a game synonymous with mom's absence.

No one ever knew; Ngquku had sworn me to silence.

The winemaker tasted the grapes from his vineyard.

This was procedural for the proper upkeep of the orchard.

Four long months later upon his death in the coal mine

No one understood how my tearless eyes said a prolonged,

Good morning sunshine, goodnight Gethsemane,

She falls silent as her thoughts are projected.

Naomi's V. Voice

O! Life can be an agonising journey!

I see I am not blessed among many.

On the near horizons happiness does not loom.

On the far this bitter-apple life epitomises gloom.

Assuming you are sane, look what you have become;

Louse-poor in a dung-sodden Nqadu Village,
And mask-smiling in the arms of a vestige.
This consuming dusk I couldn't foresee coming
Devoured my damask and spikenard life.
Thank Providence Nqadu Village is a hide-out.
This is not a fêted homecoming of an albatross.
Shameless roots! How you mistreat a home-comer!

A slight pause. Naomi looks about.

The shrine is clean, time I fetched the rain-stopper.
How daunting it is to be of threefold value to a man;
An acolyte, his sight and a customary junior wife.
Naomi, upstart girl, at least you are well and alive,
Though you've become a pierced shadow of yourself.
The future you spelt in calligraphic vainglory
To beget what you have become now, a relic.
Call the gods of your choice, offer them incense or
garlic
Blatantly hope against dispiriting hopelessness
But the ramparts are raised and high like masts.
You're not the Phoenix; from these ashes you won't rise.

Exit NAOMI *with the broom. A long interlude of bird cries ensues.*
The approaching sound of a gourd-rattle increases from a distance
off-stage. Re-enter NAOMI *leading a mildly groping* SANGOMA
SIGCAWU MANGCOTYWA. *She is rattling the gourd for his*
benefit and carrying a small pot of beer. The SANGOMA *is*
wrapped in blue and white cloths, barefoot and carrying an animal
tail wand and a snuff container. She leads him to the grave and sits
on the bare ground, leaving him towering. Stopping the rattling, she
ululates thrice sharply and claps her hands in supplication for a
moment and gradually kills the clapping. The SANGOMA *endures*
a bout of coughing, casts snuff on the grave and bursts out in rhetoric.

Mangcotywa

(Addressing the grave in lamentation)

Where are the streams that frothed down from the
hills?
This land, once famous for the lush of green meadows

That blazed with the yellow of coniferous dandelions
Is now a barren fell nourishing accusations and ills.
Did you send us rain clouds on the backs of chameleons?
Row on row of staked farmland terraced in formation
The sound of cascading rivers sang like melodeons
In eye-catching splendour towards the floors of the valleys.
Back then this beauty was the cherished Xhosa homeland
Home of pineapple, chicory, coffee and water melons.
The people hate me more than they hated *Nongqawuse*.
Be amused when they take up arms against your medium.
Inflaming liberty now prevails over sanity, great ancestor!
Of ignominy the AmaRharhabe accuse me baselessly.
From all the ridges a hubbub piques me relentlessly.
While here in tranquillity you lie and partake of libation.
Their unveiled curses hurt more than the piercing of quills.
Arise from your slumber, great AmaRharhabe spirit!
Ah! My ancestor, Zwelinzima! Shepherd of rain clouds!
Save the Xhosa from this macabre drought and famine.
Your AmaRharhabe no longer know the smell of red ochre.
Can a single upright man carry the nudity of a tribe?
Be the elephant-hide shield to shelter me from the diatribe.
This accursed drought has roused whirlwinds against me!
From Nqadu Great Palace, Gcaleka, King of the AmaXhosa,

Bellows and broadcasts scathing displeasure with this
Oracle.
The lips of Maxhobakhawuleza, King of the
AmaRharhabe,
Right-hand-son descendant of Chief Phalo the Great
Call for my eviction if rain clouds continue to abscond.
From the Western Cape, King Khoesan Cornelius
roars.
Raise men among these unthankful villains to second
Me in my innocence when they plot evil against me.
This drought deathly blankets three leonine kingdoms.
Diviners, augurs and soothsayers of the three kings
Connived against me and this Oracle to apportion
blame.
Now from the land's nonentities; the commoner and
the lame,
I endure verbal abuse and torrents of vile accusations!

Coughing and nauseatingly clearing phlegm from his throats, the
SANGOMA *kneels and casts more snuff on the grave. He clicks*
his fingers and NAOMI *gives him the pot.* SANGOMA
MANGCOTYWA *pours a sorghum brew on the grave in a dribble*
as NAOMI *clasps softly.*

Naomi

(Clapping her hands in supplication)

Ah! My ancestor, Zwelinzima! Shepherd of rain
clouds!
I implore you, in humility and sincerity
Ah! Great one with one foot in the clouds!
Ah! Great one with the other in the earth!
There is uproar, likely to end in further calamity.
Garner the spirits of reposing royalty and with one
voice
Solicit the intervention of *Qamata* in his Heavenly
Quarters.

NAOMI *stops clapping, ululates thrice and sits on her haunches in*
a very humble posture. The SANGOMA *stops pouring beer on the*

111

grave and slowly smears snuff on the skull stuck in the pole, coughing and noisily clearing his throat.

Naomi's V. Voice

(*Naomi, wistfully, looking at him*)

Wish I could find a burrow and hide myself.
To think this awry, wiry, wry and dry hoary man,
This stinking, coughing, wheezing, catarrh-spitting object,
This nondescript medicine-men, demon-keeper and destroyer,
This collection of veins and animated dry bones,
Is my husband, is ever an unwelcome realisation.
Looking into his cataract-clouded eyes, I suffer self-pity.
If there was a land of nothing but sprawling catacombs
And I could catapult this enigma of a husband
Or the mere thought of his being my spouse.
Perhaps I could be Naomi again at least in my mind.
It could've been better if I'd remained in Johannesburg
And resorted to dope for addiction and an endless stupor.
Perhaps the plumes of heroin would've blurred the shadow.

Mangcotywa

Ah! My ancestor, Zwelinzima! Shepherd of rain clouds!
You turn your face from me; are you in cahoots with evil?
My eyeballs are sprayed with venom and doused in bile!
The Chief has rallied the scum of the tribe against me!
Like a veldt fire hooligans rage against your chosen.
Shameless paedophile! They curse on anthills in the open.

This vitriol! This reversal of roles! This ugly diatribe
Forbear, as you sail on the crests that bind the Xhosa
Pray I this: that you bid and decree its death forthwith.
Lion! Prowl on the prairies; do not repose in the earth!
O! Chief Phalo, great ancestor, ominous on every
wind,
Would I this land defile knowingly, being its
benefactor?
From generations archaic hitherto the Rain Oracle
Has favoured my lineage. It is unfounded in our
existence
From time immemorial to this day, that a *sangoma*
Can be plotted against and made an object of public
ridicule.
Shamelessly you connive with the commoner.
Why did you bestow me with perishable honour?
Can a man, notable or ignoble, carry the nudity of a
tribe?
Did I err by letting paediatric eyes see my nakedness?
Was it not your hand that divinely brought her to me?
If I am guilty of ignominy, you being its architects,
Jut from the earth and accept blame with manliness.
If indeed I am covered in faeces as publicly alleged,
Is the Great Fish River inadequate for my cleansing?
Did a divine gift from *Qamata* Himself, the Ageless
Ever hoard calamity for the three basking kingdoms?
Slight pause. Then speaks in a voice weighed with rage.
I have smeared you with snuff, which is not our custom
But to shame you and sour your rest in the interim.
Resign me all you want to dejection and dismal abuse,
But though I am a speck, against you I can raise a
storm!
For three years I called your name, humble and
solicitous.
For three years daily I approached you with snuff and
beer.

For three years daily child, man and cattle fell side by side.

How remorseless of you who repose and enjoy libation!

Suddenly, startling NAOMI, *the* SANGOMA *rises, the pot of beer in his hands. He smashes it on the grave in unsurpassable fury. As the pot shatters* NAOMI *screams fearfully, jumps to her feet and backs away in disbelief. From now on* MANGCOTYWA'S *countenance is a frowning mask and his fingers open and clench.*

Naomi

(*Terrified; her hands on her chest*)

Eee! *Sangoma*! You invite the wrath of the spirits!

Mangcotywa

(*Rises a silencing hand sharply and continues riotously*)

Now my supplication to you falls and my wrath rises!

May *Qamata* pique you the way I am piqued relentlessly!

Know no peace until you have thwarted this calamity!

This alleged rain-stopper begat again as the Xhosa rainmaker

Whose accolades are sung in the Eastern and Western Cape.

This wretched day I tender my unwavering petition:

From the majestic lips of the three unconquerable kings;

Gcaleka, Maxhobakhawuleza and Cornelius, the mountains

Let praise poetry flow in my honour before the week ends.

Turn a deaf ear at your risk; now I've turned hostile!

This tranquillity and libation you enjoy undeservedly,

I'll wreck and shatter with an all-ages Xhosa anathema!

You shall be perpetually soured, in agony and restless.

Deuced, you indeed shall be, because your appeal to *Qamata*

114

The ultimate Redeemer I'll barricade with syringa
thorns!

*In a stupor of anger he gropes about for a while, gets hold of the
skull, uproots and casts it on the grave, clicking his tongue in anger.*
NAOMI, *more terrified now, slowly backs away.* SANGOMA
MANGCOTYWA *continues to desecrate the grave with his hands
and feet. Finally he fumbles with his cloths in a determined bid to
urinate on the grave. Exit* NAOMI *hurriedly, hands clasped behind
her head.*

Curtain

SCENE TWO

Midday the same day
Outside the *sangoma's* homestead consultation hut

MANGCOTYWA, *pensive, is seated on a hewn low wooden stool near a rustic door to a dilapidated hut of mortar and poles. He is in the same attire and still wears a frowning face. The ground around him is dusty and littered with paraphernalia ranging from stools, stones, broken pots etc, etc.*

Mangcotywa

(*To the door which is ajar*)
      Nondwe! Nondwe!
NAOMI, *still in the same torn dress, sticks out her head through the doorway.*
      AmaRharhabe conspirators vie for our expulsion and blood.
      I smell it in my nostrils and must be ready for engagement.
      My ancestors were vanguards of Phalo's royal regiment;
      This feat theirs in that era of Xhosa unity which I glimpse.
      My forebears were the bodyguard of Chief Phalo the Great.
      In my veins flows bravery and thirst for the sight of blood.
      Every Xhosa I can bludgeon if the sun would stand still!
      Fetch me all my weapons; soon I'll disembowel my enemies.

Naomi

(*Curtseying and bringing hands together in humility*)
      Sangoma, you mean *all* your weapons?

Mangcotywa

I mean it, Nondwe. Those your eyes can see,
For I have both visible and invisible weaponry,
Weaponry deadlier than a rinderpest pestilence
To render lame, to render insane, to render death!

NAOMI *fully emerges from the hut and walks across the dreary yard. Exit NAOMI. She re-enters carrying a heavy cluster of an assortment of traditional battle weapons bundled together with a band. She places them at his feet where he is pointing and kneels nearby, curious, fearful and expectant of further instructions. He quickly unties the bundle and draws out two short spears.*

(In admiration, fingering the edge of the blades)

Izikempe spear... for stabbing and killing.

Ijozi spear...for jabbing, tearing and killing.

These conspirators! What can hasten them?

(Pause)

Fetch my hunting rifle, men must fall in clusters!
This is the one-warrior regiment that routs regiments!
For years I vainly craved peace with the Xhosa, being Xhosa
May the spirits reward my mongering for war this day,
To rout both the AmaXhosa and the AmaRharhabe.

Exit NAOMI. *Meanwhile* MANGCOTYWA *quickly picks the array of weaponry and spreads it around him, placing two long spears and a knobkerrie against the wall behind him. Re-enter* NAOMI, *gingerly bearing a long old hunting rifle. She registers disbelief at the manner and swiftness with which he has spread the weaponry. He takes the gun and blows dust off it, his face twisted in a mirthless rictus of a smile. Using a handkerchief, he begins to wipe the gun.*

(Wiping the gun)

Fetch me Thoshla; I must have conference.

Exit NAOMI *into the consultation hut.* MANGCOTYWA *disassembles the rifle and starts to dust, blow and wipe its components. He finds one long bullet in the chamber and wedges it between his ear and temple.* NAOMI *re-enters bearing, waiter-like, a gourd totally covered in beadwork on a small reed tray. He waves her back rudely.*

> *Gcau-n*! I said Thoshla, Nondwe! That is Clara!
> Do not confuse their cordial-seeming kinship;
> Though they hunger and thirst, giggle and grimace
> When they thirst for water and kindly request it
> And in your quest to experiment you give them vinegar,
> They will fold you up sixteen-fold like a napkin.
> Or fall on you like a sledgehammer on a Coca-Cola can;
> Among other things wrath is coiled in them like adders!

NAOMI *quickly exits. He shakes his head pityingly and resumes cleaning the components with quick, jerky movements. Re-enter* NAOMI *with another gourd, also heavily beaded, but distinctly different in colour. A long string emanates from the gourd. She places the tray among the weaponry and takes her position.*

One hand holding the stock of the rifle, he picks the tray and rattles the gourd noisily until it seems to gyrate with momentum. After a while of rattling showmanship he sets the tray down and plugs the end of the string into his ear and listens, frozen, head inclined at an angle, nodding occasionally. Moments pass and he begins to assemble the rifle. All the while, NAOMI'S *eyes are riveted on him.*

> Something is brewing, rumbling underground.
> Something evil and something good will happen this week.
> I hear of a grave whose occupant Thoshla dreads to disclose.
> I hear of a wedding whose bride and bridegroom are mismatched.
> It cannot be us, not on account of the mismatch
> But because Thoshla tells me I am worse than dandruff to you.

He scherzos a litany for your dissatisfaction and
disaffection
Being sympathetic of your person and your
vulnerability.
Refute this irrefutable truth, Nondwe. Refute it now.

Naomi
(Caught off-guard, she shrugs and sits in the dust)
He speaks the truth, *Sangoma*. But no options exist.

Mangcotywa
I have always known that you do not love me,
Nondwe.
Gcau-u! How would you when everyone abhors me?
The commoner, royalty and the dead have turned
virulent.
When you returned to the Cape three years ago
You were a pathetic calabash of nightmares and
hysteria.
Two evils beleaguered you; a shadow and gonorrhoea.
Ostracised, penniless and ailing, you verged on
dementia.
Though there was breath in you, you were dead,
Nondwe.
The city spat you out like cud, and you returned to
the Cape
An ailing mother of one, a murderess and a fugitive.
But your own kith and kin turned you away on sight.
Your son is six years old now but refuses to call me
father.
You do not seem thankful that I am raising your son.

Naomi
Please, leave Vincent out of this painful conversation.
But my son and I only looked for shelter, *Sangoma*.
I had resolved to surrender to the police for the
interview.
I was not a suspect and the police were not charging me.

The authorities sought only to interview me for some leads.

I am not a murderess and I am not a wanted fugitive.

Mangcotywa

Then what are you doing in this anomalous village?

Why are you enduring mosquito bites in Nqadu?

Anyway, what anchors you to my homestead?

On what basis are you serving my spirits with distinction?

Take Vincent to the city and enrol him at a kindergarten.

In Johannesburg is sumptuous exotic food to be partaken

And luxurious garden flats to be occupied.

Go, Nondwe, the city beckons, what binds you?

Naomi

If I cross any river terrible woes assail me again.

The last time it happened seven Smuts stalked me.

Mangcotywa

My herbs, concoctions and hands cleansed you clean.

Daily I bathed your body and prayed for your exoneration.

The spirits and the gods were reluctant but they bowed.

Soon the allegation of murder was no longer whispered

The manhunt was called off and the reward cancelled.

I placed my honour on the anvil and resurrected you.

My two wives and seventeen children deserted me!

The AmaXhosa and the AmaRharhabe are at war with me.

From the dead you are now risen, I can see, Nondwe.

And in appreciation you honour me with disaffection!

If it were dissatisfaction alone perchance I would understand;

Years of demonic indulgence have weakened my virility.

Blood was on your hands and you were on the verge
of insanity.
I cleansed you of a white man's shadow that had
displaced yours.
Thank your recommendations for the past three years.
You resigned yourself to serving me and befriending
my gourds.
You sang for the goblins heartily and kept the shrine
tidy.

Naomi

But I've been faithful all these three years, *Sangoma*,
Despite tantrums, a punitive impotence on your part,
And the penultimate conjugality with the goblins.

Mangcotywa

It is uncustomary for a Xhosa man to call a woman
wife
When the *mpothulo*, the *inghakhwe* and the *ubulunga* cow;
The imperative cows for a wedding and a blessed
marriage,
Have not been delivered and *lobola* has not been paid.
Even if we were in agreement who would receive the
lobola
When both your parents are departed and survived
by ravens?
I wanted to live with you till the end of my days,
Nondwe.
But this is not a penitentiary and I am not a prison
warden.

*He pulls the string from his ear and quickly finishes assembling the
gun. Appraising the gun, he begins to speak slowly, contemplatively.*

If I let you go the white man's shadow will bother
you again.
The police will resume searching for you, Nondwe.
And dementia will overtake you within the week.
If I let you stay I consign the Xhosas to their graves.

Naomi

It's within your abilities to arrest my woes
permanently.
By the ankle you hold me, my head suspended in a
furnace.
When do I regain my freedom and my old self again?
Within I feel self-estranged and wonder if I am not a
gourd.
Perhaps it's an illusion that I am still alive, *Sangoma*.
When I converse with Thoshla, Clara and the others
They hint to me we appear like quadruplets.

*He aims the gun with both hands at a distant target and appears set
to pull the trigger, but looks at her and smiles, placing the gun across
his lap.*

Mangcotywa

You need me now more than ever before, Nondwe.
Initially, only one figure of the Commissioner stalked
you.
Now you are at the mercy of a legion Commissioners;
All of them suave replicas of the ghost that haunted
you.
They're now in my employ that is how I fenced you
inside.
They're here, a quiet and attentive audience as we
speak,
Only awaiting orders like any other Commissioners.

NAOMI *shakes her head and begins to cry, looking in his eyes,
vainly appealing for pity. After a long while he slowly holds out a
hand as if stopping a truck. He leans towards her.*

There is something I need from you in exchange for
the world.
Vanguards of armies are closing in around me inch
by inch.
Thoshla has vowed to repel them but demands warm
blood.

123

MANGCOTYWA *picks the gun from his lap and rises, he stretches and yawns, raising and lowering the rifle in an almost leisurely fashion. Stooping, he says in weary tones, holding out an empty hand towards her as though to receive something.*

> That coloured boy, that Vincent of yours, who is hardly here,
> That boy who refuses to call me father is your ticket to the future.
> In exchange of a more promising city life give me that boy.

NAOMI *looks at him in shock. A moment of staring passes. Suddenly the SANGOMA glances from side to side as if searching for something, then cups a hand around his ear and listens. The booming drone of an arriving jeep reaches them. Quickly he aims the rifle off-stage above NAOMI in the direction of the drone. The drone is swallowed by the noise of revs as the jeep comes to a halt off-stage. The noise of the engine dies and a brief silence is preceded by a car door slamming and the shriek of a security alarm system engaging. NAOMI turns and caps her eyes with her hand. MANGCOTYWA swiftly cocks the rifle and maintains a steady aim, an eye closed, ready to discharge.*

> Someone is coming, a collaborator of the conspirators! The AmaRharhabe send their harbinger of war, Nondwe!

Naomi

(*Fearfully*)
> Yes, a man is coming, *Sangoma!*

Promptly NAOMI rises and dashes into the consultation room and sticks her head out through the doorway, alternately looking at the SANGOMA and in the direction the vehicular noise came from. Enter a jaded BONGINKOSI carrying a travelling bag and the leather duffel bag, now old and worn out. He is emaciated and not as lustrous as before. He is in mountain-safari hiking attire; khaki cargo pants, a matching shirt and a sleeveless cargo vest. On seeing the gun aimed at him BONGINKOSI freezes momentarily, then slowly puts the bags down and raises his hands in surrender.

Bonginkosi

Sakubona, Sangoma! *Sakubona,* Great Seer!

Excuse the lack of announcement, *Sangoma.*

But I pray that you see my innocence and harmlessness.

I come in peace, Great Seer, and I… I bear a letter for you.

Mangcotywa

Who are you, stranger? Plainly state your business!

The battle lines are drawn, evil precursor, and you stutter!

Bonginkosi

I… I am Bonginkosi, a gored Zulu from Johannesburg.

I've come to consult the great Oracle, *Sangoma* Sigcawu

Mangcotywa, revered custodian of the AmaRharhabe Oracle.

It takes a while of appraisal before the SANGOMA *slowly lowers the barrel and beckons him to approach.* BONGINKOSI *picks his bags and approaches the* SANGOMA *slowly, briefly marvelling at the displayed weaponry.*

Mangcotywa

(*To Naomi*)

Gcau-u! Fetch a stool for the Zulu luminary!

NAOMI'S *head vanishes into the consultation hut momentarily. She re-enters with a low hewn stool, which she sets on the ground for* BONGINKOSI. *The* SANGOMA *sits after the visitor has set his bags down and taken the stool.* NAOMI *sits on the threshold of the consultation hut.* MANGCOTYWA *speaks in sorrow, by way of apologising for the fright* BONGINKOSI *suffered.*

You come at a terrible, terrible time, Bonginkosi;

A heart-souring time when Xhosa draws *ijozi* against Xhosa

A heart-wrenching time indeed in the history of the tribe.

Bonginkosi

(Draws a sealed khaki envelope from his jacket)
> A terrified state messenger from Bisho is outside.

> He begged me on his knees to hand you this envelope.
MANGCOTYWA *nods at* NAOMI *who takes the envelope from*
BONGINKOSI *and returns to sit on the threshold, already reading
the address on the envelope.*

Naomi

(Reading the address)
> **To: *Sangoma* Sigcawu Mangcotywa; c/o Nqadu
> Post Office**
> Nqadu Village, Eastern Cape.

*Quickly she opens the envelope and draws out an annexed typed
letter. She reads aloud:*
> **From: The Deputy Premier, Hon. Mr Ralph
> Ngakane Nqoko;
> Eastern Cape Provincial Office, Bisho.**

> **Ref: Borehole drilling at Nqadu Village.**

She looks at Mangcotywa
> It is written in English, *Sangoma.*

Mangcotywa

(Angrily)
> *Gcau-u*! Read it!

Naomi

(Resumes reading aloud the letter)

> **Dear *Sangoma*.**

> **Be informed that following aerial surveys
> conducted in the Eastern
> Cape Province by the Department of Water
> Engineering in the Ministry of Water Affairs and
> Land Development, a large body of underground
> water was discovered precisely below your**

Nqadu Shrine and homestead. That being the case, you are now required pursuant of the Law and Statutory Instrument 901 of 2009 to relocate your shrine and homestead to pave way for the proposed drilling and permanent establishment of the much needed borehole and aquifers at that place for the benefit of all Nqadu Villagers and their livestock.

You are to relocate within seven days from the date stamped on this notice. Take notice that a statutory instrument is an act of Parliament; hence this notice to relocate is incontestable in the Magistrate's Court except by meritorious urgent application to the High Court of South Africa weighted by King Maxhobakhawuleza-endorsed merits offering a feasible and popular alternative. Should you elect to resist, you are required by Law to file such application with the Registrar of the High Court at Pretoria within seven days of receipt of this notice. Further, take notice that upon expiry of the seven-day period, should you oppose by default riotous force may be used against you. However, this office does not expect opposition from you as it would be an act of sabotage for you to do so and retrogressive to oppose community development and the government.

Kindly contact the Director of the Department of National Archives and Archaeology for possible assistance with exhumation. The Director of the Ministry of Transport awaits your instructions to transport your belongings. The Ministry of Social Welfare stands ready to assist you provisionally should destitution threaten.

Kindly append your signature to the annexed affidavit as proof of your having received this notice.

Thank you in advance for your understanding and cooperation.

Yours faithfully, Signature, Hon. Ralph Ngakane Nqoko.
Cc: The Provincial Premier, Eastern Cape, South Africa
Cc: His Royal Highness, King Maxhobakhawuleza
Cc: *Sangoma* Hilarious Idutywa, Chairperson of CONTRALESA
Cc: Ass. Comm. Sachwayo Ntini, Police Commander, Eastern Cape

Mangcotywa

(*Casually, sniffing snuff unperturbed*)
Read it again, Nondwe, loudly and slowly.
NAOMI *reads the main body of the letter again. As she does* MANGCOTYWA *detachedly busies himself with the rifle and the weapons around him; restlessly arranging and rearranging them, while* BONGINKOSI *just sits forlorn.* NAOMI *holds out the papers.*
What is the letter saying, Nondwe?

Naomi

I am afraid it's a terrible message, *Sangoma.*

Mangcotywa

Do not tell me what you think, young virago!
Tell me in plain terms what the letter is saying.

Naomi

I am afraid eviction... government-backed expulsion. The government is taking over the shrine and homestead.

They say it is on account of the severity of the drought.

Now they have given us seven days to vacate Nqadu. You are to acknowledge receipt by signing the attached affidavit.

MANGCOTYWA *looks at her aghast, and then rises slowly, but energetically thrusts out a hand towards* NAOMI. *She jumps to her feet and dashes to give him the documents and backs away to the threshold. Holding the gun under his armpit,* MANGCOTYWA *looks at the papers, flipping through them.*

Mangcotywa

(*Voice quaking with rage, arms quavering. Skywards*)
I am Mangcotywa, I cannot be commanded!
My command comes from the earth, not Pretoria!
Sanctified by spirits, no man can desecrate me!
Neither man nor spirits can evict me from this shrine!
O Charisma of self-perpetuating evil miasma!
How you unite amaXhosa to perish in an enigma!

He tears the documents into quarters and casts them into the air over BONGINKOSI. *As the pieces of paper float to the ground, he removes the bullet from the chamber, crosses to the baffled visitor and thrusts the bullet into the dumbfounded* BONGINKOSI'S *hand, and points at the pieces of paper.*

This, my signature, hand over to the messenger outside!

BONGINKOSI *promptly picks the pieces of paper and runs outside. Exit* BONGINKOSI. MANGCOTYWA *paces the yard like a caged lion. Re-enter* BONGINKOSI *in humility and resumes his seat. The* SANGOMA *continues to pace for a while, occasionally roaring, occasionally mimicking war and gesturing curses. His chest heaving, he sits on his stool and mutely plugs the goblin string into his ear again, the gun across his lap. Nodding, he appraises an unsettled* BONGINKOSI *who nervously removes his shoes, shoves the duffel bag towards the* SANGOMA *and sits cross-legged in the dust. Exit* NAOMI *into the consultation hut. She re-emerges with a large wooden plate, which she sets between the two men, and returns to sit on the threshold.* MANGCOTYWA *speaks, looking at* BONGINKOSI *intently, but his voice is calmer.*

The sky shut her bowels and the earth's surface cracked.
The rain-god habitually withdraws services to extol obeisance
Hunger illuminates the importance of satisfaction
Suffice to say, faceless guilt adorns innocence.
Death, the masquerade, is the importance of life and its essence.
But on anthills fools barricade reason and parade ignorance.
Nudity is in the fray now because intercourse preoccupies man
My eyes have seen the eyeballs of gods and spirits of all ages.
Colour-blind gods do not perceive foreskins, virginity or blood.
This threesome is the all-time blindness of all races and ages.
Guiltlessness, the feeling thereof, not innocence, assuages gods.
You have suffered too much bereavement and are leg-weary
Here is a *sangoma* overnight man-made into an evil enigma.
Bonginkosi, your salvation I have it in my custody right here.
But lend ear, recalcitrant descendent of *impi* warriors.
BONGINKOSI *draws a large banknote from his pocket, crouches to the wooden plate and deposits it inside. From the duffel bag he removes the gourd nervously and sets it near the wooden plate. He crouches back to his position.*

Bonginkosi

(*His head tilted, his hands clasped in humility*)

I have globe-trotted and suffered and am battle-weary.
Sangoma, name your cattle and unburden me of this evil.
For seven years my life has agonised me night and day.
Death, misfortune, and disharmony rage like a wildfire.
My wealth, my people, my manhood, my esteem are gone.

Mangcotywa

Zulu boy, you come at a time when I don't need money.
You come at a time when I am warring with men and spirits.
My rainmaking ancestors need chilli to incite the rain-god.
They need rare ambrosia and a constant reminder in the shrine.
All Cape rivers would sparkle again and the rift would mend.
Make my rivers meander and I will put blood in your veins.
The reins of all things earthly and godly are in my palms.
By choice I could rain death and ruin on both men and gods.
Give me the capability to spread reign to the two worlds.

Bonginkosi

I am listening, *Sangoma*. What would it take to unburden me?

Mangcotywa

The spirits lax and slumber as the world crumbles on me.
The head of an albino child is your salvation, Bonginkosi.

131

BONGINKOSI *holds his head in disbelief as* MANGCOTYWA *rises, ending the consultation.* NAOMI *shakes her head in pity as the curtain closes.*

Curtain

SCENE THREE

Midday
Second day. Outside the *sangoma's* homestead
consultation hut

The setting and props are largely the same as the previous scene with the exception of the absence of the weapons. NAOMI, in another worn-out dress and still as unkempt as she was the day before, is squatting and grinding herbs with a grindstone, sweat running down her face and temples. Several small woven baskets and trays full of twigs, roots, tubers and tree leaves are on the ground to her left. To her right are several containers containing what she has ground. She is humming and engrossed in the grinding with no strain showing on her face.

In a far corner is a very bored BONGINKOSI sitting on an old wooden chair and wearily watching NΛOMI perform the chore. The duffel bag is between his feet near a battered enamel cup and dinner plate with remains of thick bulga porridge. BONGINKOSI rises and lazily walks away. Exit BONGINKOSI. NAOMI continues to grind without taking notice. Re-enter, a while later, BONGINKOSI carrying two cans of Coca-Cola and two large packets of potato crepes. He crosses to NAOMI and towers above her. But NAOMI continues to grind unabated. He shakes his head and places one packet on the grinding rock, followed by a can. NAOMI stops grinding and looks up at him.

Bonginkosi
(Backing away to sit on the chair)
> You're thirsty and hungry, I'm no goof; you need a roof.
> It's been a while since we last had vinegar-spiced bulga.
> And ceaselessly you work, like an automaton and shadoof.

What flows in your veins, blood or the River Volga?
He sinks onto the chair. NAOMI, *frozen watches him. They stare at each other for a moment, then* NAOMI *gazes at the packet and the can on the rock. She picks up the packet delicately, appraises it, and smiles as if recognition has dawned. She does the same with the can of Coca-Cola. She sits in the dirt, hastily opening the containers, a small smile on her face. But tears roll down her cheeks.*

Naomi
It jolts my mind with flashes of civilisation
Of a seemingly joyous, yet sad life once lived,
A trendy life of elation once experienced,
A vintage *Alfasad* once owned and driven,
Blinding Pope-beatifying beauty once monopolised.
I am popped popcorn on red embers, compromised.
But my mouth is tomb-sealed against talk nostalgic.
My past and everything I went through is lethargic.
My thoughts roam cul-de-sacs, restless and nomadic.

Bonginkosi
Like a concentration camp slave-labourer you work,
But looking around there is no garrison or bulwark.

Naomi
(*Ponderously*)
Are you asking how I coursed myself in these things?
My mind is shut, I think not of a thousand things.
I lack the thoughts to think of a thousand things.
I ignore poverty and the false spectre of poverty.
Both stand tall and proud for forbidding acrimony
And suggest a gloomy Judas-pursuit of money.
I content myself in the arena of pleasant levity.
Thought things reason falsely that wealth is essential
For a person to be a veritable person of sound mind.
In this domain of masquerades hindrances abound
Which seduce vagabonds to kill in pursuit of the pound.
So, when walking, I walk. When pounding, I pound.
When grinding, I grind. When grinning, I grin.

Walking; I walk on towards the burning bush.
Oblivious of the walking, the bush and the walker.
That is the discourse of my coursing in these things.
But I must drive you away; leave before it's too late.
BONGINKOSI *looks at her quizzically. He is perplexed. She begins to eat and drink.*

Bonginkosi

If destruction awaits me here, then here I shall die.
At this homestead I perish or the death warrant is erased.
My horoscope says Pluto will be moving towards Jupiter.
A rare phenomenon; it means I shall be unburdened here.

Naomi

Present the said albino and the planets shall repel.
Like a lunatic, to your own heart you wield a scalpel.
This is a place of woes and their hosting to the apex.
Now you are on despair's summit, at you death pecks.

Bonginkosi

But my gods-favoured horoscope does not fabricate.
May I ask: what brought you to this purgatory, Nondwe?

Naomi

Smut. Police Comm. Stuart van Smut, the eerie Boer.
I dispatched the officer on an errand to the Indian Ocean.
For four fugitive years I lived like a rat in the city's alleys.

Bonginkosi

(Pitifully)

No, Nondwe. He disappeared long ago,
Perhaps as a stowaway in a ship's Tokyo-bound cargo.

Naomi

You were not exhaustive in your search for a solution.
Now your senses have been arrested; your dialogue is bland.

135

And your diction is poetic like that of Thoshla and Roshtoto.

Bonginkosi
Thoshla and Roshtoto, who are they?

Naomi
Powerful residents I know. Never mind, Bonginkosi.

Bonginkosi
Of late I flew to Samye Temple in the Himalayas.
Upon my arrival monks and Lamas sounded cymbals
And blew big-belled trumpets to chase any demons
That might have stalked me from the depths of Africa.
Placed I the gourd, now turned cactus, before Lama Iyasa
This at night in a monastery shrouded in deep silence.
Guilty felt I, afraid I had brought the Tibetans a pestilence.
Time lapsed, yet the Lama uttered no word, like a mute.
Cross-legged we sat, between us the tacit brute.
Then asked Iyasa: what is it with this heartless flower?
That can dement and destroy an African at any hour?
Inconsolable you lumber like a rhinoceros castaway.
Endlessly in the mundane realm you dangerously sway
From the age-old tranquil and meritorious Middle Way.
Nirvana is the sound of one hand clapping in the Void.
It summons all beings to place themselves in the Fold.
Eight elevated candles did high-born Lama Iyasa light,
Ceaselessly pleading with me in reason not to delight.
The guru informed me he had thwarted my karma.
The karma and the goblin were now non-existent anathema.
Lo! Empty-handed I left the monastery like one in a drama
My mind burdened with unlocking the Tibetan mystery.

But, alas, on getting to Johannesburg, there in the
pantry,
Mesmerising and unmistaken like old Chinese tapestry
Stood the leafless plant, turning into a gourd again,
Irrefutable evidence of an assurance void and vain.

Naomi

Globetrotting is not synonymous with agonising
passion.
As yet you suffer the suffering your relations suffered.
The sworn witness and the tallying officer of the
crucified
That is your category like that of a UN Observer
Mission.
Now you turn the tables and present yourself for
crucifixion.

Bonginkosi

Less than an eighth of my inheritance remains now.
The bestial estate consumed people and itself before
my eyes.
My stay is an appeal for an alternative method of
payment.
I do solicit your support to convince him to accept
the jeep.
The yet-to-be deer-hunted and beheaded innocent
albino
Abroad on the lullaby plains, perhaps Xhosa, perhaps
Zulu
Ought to be allowed to live, but virulent death put to
sleep.

Suddenly, from off-stage, comes a growing noise of the SANGOMA's
coughs and catarrh-spitting. NAOMI *quickly throws the can and
the crepes at* BONGINKOSI *and resumes her chores; grinding
and humming. Enter* SANGOMA MANGCOTYWA *near*
NAOMI, *his face ferocious and his disposition war-like. He is
wrapped in red cloths and barefoot. The gun is strap-slung across his*

back. His hands and feet are soiled. He carries a sack and a digging pick which, halting, he drops on the ground as he appears. Grabbing the bottom of the sack, teeth gritted, he rolls a human skull across the yard towards BONGINKOSI *who jumps to his feet in terror.*

Mangcotywa

(*He bellows pointing at the rolling skull*)

There! My ancestor; Mfilu Tutu Zwelinzima's skull!
The grave is dug, empty and yearns for your recompense!
Yet you sit like one awaiting the *Mapungubwe* award!
Is it conferred on he whose sword has rusted in its scabbard?

NAOMI *rises, terror-stricken beside a chest-heaving* MANGCOTYWA. *A long, tense moment of silence and uncertainty passes.*

Bonginkosi

We must talk, Sangoma; I am offering the jeep.

Mangcotywa

Gcau-u! Uncouth! Undomesticated, uninitiated Zulu boy!
You come like Chaka's *impi* to belittle my great ancestor!
You equate a low-cost jeep with feared Zwelinzima's skull!
Gcau-u! You rouse my fury beyond words, Zulu boy!
Gcau!

Naomi

(*To Bonginkosi, appealingly*):

Recompense or you court calamity.
He will marry you to untold misery and dejection.
This –your rejection for your salvation
Is your acceptance of a fate irreversible.
Upon arrival, head held high, you looked responsible
Now there you stand shooting yourself in the foot.

Mangcotywa

By sunset tomorrow it shall be two albinos!
MANGCOTYWA *turns and storms away. Exit*
MANGCOTYWA, *leaving* NAOMI *and* BONGINKOSI
baffled and terrified. For a while the two stare at each other across
the yard and at the skull near BONGINKOSI'S *feet. He drops*
onto the chair and clutches his head miserably, frozen in thought.

Naomi

Find him that cursed payment he so demands.
I too am making my disbursement to him tonight.
When liberty is at stake nothing is too dear, stranger.
For freedom battalions perish in fierce combat, Bongi.
NAOMI *watches him for a moment, then begins to walk slowly*
towards him. A pace from him, she stops and is about to shake his
shoulder when she looks over him off-stage and is momentarily
petrified. She yells once, holding her head, and silently retreats slowly,
eyes bulging in shock, prompting BONGINKOSI *to look in the*
direction in which she is gazing. Staring off-stage, he gapes and he
rises. The two retreat and halt near the door of the consultation hut,
their stares still fixed off-stage.
Enter a rural teenager ushering FR BRYN FLYNN. *The*
teenager *quickly turns and exits.* FR FLYNN *is in polished shoes,*
a dark suit, a purple shirt, a large crucifix and a priest's collar; his
elegance is in sharp contrast to the dreary environment. FR FLYNN
halts and also stares at them. FR FLYNN'S *face is bland and his*
bearing exudes reserve. NAOMI *quavers, points at him then begins*
to wail loudly like one bereaved.

Fr. Flynn

(*Crosses himself. Voice cathedral*)
Open your eyes and see the falsity of the mirage.
The tumultuous Red Sea hid a passage.
Sweetness hid in the bitter water at Mara.
Daily for forty years Israel was bitten.
Daily for forty years the House of Israel was smitten.
Of creation is it not written:
Out of darkness light came out?

You who cry, what Egyptian armies surround you?
NAOMI *staggers across to him, falls at his feet and grabs them. Prone and clinging to his ankles, she kicks and cries like a helpless child.*
Enter SOGO *carrying an exquisite trunk and the Holy Bible. He is smartly dressed in gentlemanly attire, neat and butler-like in bearing.* SOGO *delicately places the trunk on the ground and dutifully stands beside* FR FLYNN. SOGO *draws a handkerchief from his breast pocket and gives it to the priest.* FR FLYNN *looks down at* NAOMI *and wipes tears from his eyes. Stooping,* FR FLYNN *pats her gently at the back and draws her to her feet. She clutches the labels of his jacket and buries her sobbing face in his chest. He puts an arm around her and gently shushes her; all the while,* SOGO *is standing still and* BONGINKOSI *is staring at them in disbelief.* NAOMI, *still clutching his lapels, leans backwards and looks in his face.* FR FLYNN *shakes his head mildly.* NAOMI *lets go of him and retreats to* BONGINKOSI. FR FLYNN *wipes more tears from his face, adjusts his suit, looks about, and starts towards the wooden chair.* SOGO *quickly crosses to the chair and holds it courteously for* FR FLYNN *to sit.* SOGO *humbly stands beside the seated priest.* NAOMI *sits in the dust and* BONGINKOSI *finds a stool and sits on it. Both are near the door of the consultation hut.*
Enter blindly, on NAOMI *and* BONGINKOSI'S *side, a coloured boy of six years,* VINCENT, *and driving an imaginary car at speed. He is filthy, unkempt and in rags. Midway across the gap between the parties the boy halts fearfully upon looking up and seeing the seated* FR FLYNN *and glances at* NAOMI. FR FLYNN *stares at the boy, strokes his chin and rises, his eyes riveted on* VINCENT, *who is also staring back at him. But looking down* VINCENT *notices the skull near* FR FLYNN, *screams and runs to* NAOMI. FR FLYNN *remains on his feet, watching the boy keenly.*

Curtain

Act Four

EPILOGUE

Mid-morning
Third day. Courtyard of the *sangoma's* homestead

The yard is swept and cleared of dirt. FR FLYNN, *in another two-piece suit, is hunched on the crumbling wooden chair and engrossed in reading the Holy Bible.* VINCENT, *in clean but tattered clothes and barefoot, is sitting on the ground beside the priest, tying and untying* FR FLYNN'S *shoelace. Now and again,* FR FLYNN *ruffles* VINCENT'S *hair playfully without taking his eyes off the Bible.* NAOMI *is sprinkling the yard with water from a bucket and using a traditional broom to stop the dust rising. Her hair is combed neatly and her dress is smart and less worn out than the others. She is still barefoot.*

A cheap portable radio set is on a stool near the door of the consultation hut, its antenna extended.

Enter SOGO, *smartly dressed as before, but in different gentlemanly attire. He is carrying a small folded aluminium table, which he unfolds and sets, butler-like, before* FR FLYNN. *Briefly, he stands back and mutely appraises the waist-high table in relation to the yard, nods satisfaction to himself and walks in the direction of his entry. Exit* SOGO.

NAOMI *looks about and seems satisfied. Exit* NAOMI *with the broom and the bucket. Re-enter* NAOMI *carrying a goatskin, which she spreads about three paces from* FR FLYNN *and sits on.* FR FLYNN *remains engrossed in the Bible and* VINCENT *continues to tie and untie the priest's shoelace.*

Enter a tired-looking BONGINKOSI *in the same cargo attire.*

Bonginkosi
I walked to all the surrounding villages through reeds,
And inquired from commoners, headmen and kids,
If they had seen the seer this morning or last night,
They hadn't, but wished he had taken his flight.

Fr. Flynn

Find him, please; we need his sanction and presence.
Soon incense shall be in the air; time is of the essence.
Here we're only strangers and this is far from a synod;
Therefore we can't do anything unless he gives the nod.

Naomi

Search the riverside meadows and the northern pastures.
Angered, he stoically perambulates in serene places,
Being the paradox that he is, till the embers dim.
Coerce him with caution; angry he kills and maims.

Exit BONGINKOSI. FR FLYNN *resumes reading the Bible and stroking* VINCENT'S *head. Enter* SOGO *with the exquisite trunk and sets it on the ground near the table. From it he draws three white cloths, drapes them on his forearm and reverently spreads them one on top of the other on the table. The cloths cover the surface of the table. He sets three candlesticks in holders symmetrically on either side of the table.* SOGO *stands back to appraise the arrangement, then, one by one, he takes out a paten, a chalice and a ciborium and sets them inverted centrally between the candlesticks. Finally he draws a sealed wine bottle and a small lunchbox and places them behind the silverware, and closes the trunk. Exit* SOGO *with the trunk.*

Naomi

(*Haltingly, after much hesitation*)

But, Father, forgive the disbelief and doubt in my heart.
Though I see you with my eyes I wonder if you are real.
Is the priest I see not the ravings of my unhinged senses?
Tell me what happened in Rome, time is of the essence;
The *sangoma* is an extraordinaire at counter-attack.
This homestead is a death-trap, beware of a heart attack.

Fr. Flynn

One thing in the world God didn't give man is time.
I thank Him because the narrative would fill tomes.
But brief like the bellowed bursts of creation I shall be.
Rome welcomed me devilishly like a veteran wizard.
A scourge of bodily illness I suffered, inexplicably rashly.
For once I was persuaded and disarmed by a buzzard.
This was a sure omen for a rude descent into dishonour.
Narrowly I could have descended to Hell overburdened.
Nothing dissuaded me that the Cardinals, those bland men
Of great sobriety of speech and stature without measure,
Had decreed the forfeiture of my priesthood and future.
In Rome the Cardinals ex-communicated and disrobed me.

Naomi

O! Do not tell me you are a roving degradation!

Fr. Flynn

I countered the Cardinals with an Irish *tokoloshe*.

Naomi

What is an Irish *tokoloshe*, Father Flynn?

Fr. Flynn

An academic enigma and clangouring bombshell,
Beyond description, Naomi; hence Irish *tokoloshe*.
Seven *senseis* exchanged blows to determine sentence.
My excommunication was commuted to a year's obeisance.
I tasked a surgeon to dismember me for certain repentance.

Enter SOGO *carrying a suitcase. He has donned on top of his clothing a frilled red and white flowing robe.* VINCENT *stops tying*

145

and untying FR FLYNN'S *shoelace mesmerised by* SOGO'S *appearance. As* SOGO *approaches them, fear registers on* VINCENT'S *face. The boy rises and dashes to the door of the consultation hut, where he sits on the ground near the portable radio set.* FR FLYNN *smiles and waves at him reassuringly, then rises and puts the Bible on the chair as* SOGO *opens the suitcase at his feet. Reverently,* SOGO *takes out a red and densely frilled chasuble from the suitcase, crosses himself, and helps* FR FLYNN *don it.*

Mr Sogo, my right hand man, graduated from Oxford.
A doctor of divinity he was and lectured at Fort Hare.
The hare erred by going out of his way to attempt yoga.
Under the eyes of a deranged guru he chanted mantras.
Demons trapped him; the learned bachelor turned tramp.

Enter BONGINKOSI *with a low wooden stool as* SOGO *ceremoniously dresses* FR FLYNN. *Assuming a bearing of reverence,* BONGINKOSI *walks humbly to* NAOMI *and sits on the stool beside her and gestures a vain search. But* SOGO *gestures to the two to rise and present something before the makeshift altar. Exit* NAOMI *and* BONGINKOSI *in different directions.* VINCENT *smiles and claps his hands enthusiastically. Re-enter* NAOMI *with two large old-fashioned pots and sets them before the altar. Exit* NAOMI *into the consultation hut briefly. Re-enter* NAOMI *bearing a large reed tray laden with gourds and numerous nondescript fetish items, idols, and abstract voodoo dolls. She tips the load over the two pots.* VINCENT *smiles and claps his hands more eagerly, then checks himself. Exit* NAOMI *into the hut. Meanwhile,* SOGO *puts a white and red stole around the priest's neck. Re-enter* NAOMI *with another load of nondescript mediumistic paraphernalia, which she heaps on the others. Exit* NAOMI *through the door. Re-enter* NAOMI *carrying bundled ancestral cloths of various colours and designs, which she casts onto the growing heap.* VINCENT *rises and cheers more vigorously by clapping his hands and stamping his feet but, checking himself again, sticks out his tongue in mock embarrassment, drops to the ground beside the radio set, and begins to fidget with it. Enter* BONGINKOSI *with the duffel bag, which he places on top of the heap as* SOGO *adjusts a red amice over* FR FLYNN'S *shoulders.* NAOMI *and* BONGINKOSI *retreat and sit as before;* NAOMI *on the goatskin,* BONGINKOSI *on the low stool.* SOGO *draws a purple cincture from the suitcase and begins to wind it round* FR FLYNN'S *waistline.*

But reinstatement the Cardinals deemed impossible
Now cognisant of myself and unfathomable Africa's needs
I made urgent application to Papa for change of ministry.
Only after much prodigious fasting and prodigal prayer;
After fastidious self-denial, solitude and detachment
The ministry I am about to perform was given me by God.
For three years I was in solitary confinement in the vaults,
Seeing no one but Michael and the communion of angels.
Now I am a missile that roves the dark areas of the world.
I have tamed eunuchs and subdued the demons of vast India.
I have made spectacle of the vicious demons of Indonesia.
Now I have returned to the Rainbow Nation to render service.
Brother Sogo is irrefutable living proof of God's power;
For in the head of this once-balanced ex-Oxford don,
Demons and knowledge once vied for a common frontier.
The sophical the morons loved to hate is now my chauffer.

But the Cathedral stirred appalling images in my head.
A soporific tarpaulin lifted and I recalled a cynical past.
Guilt filled my humane chest askance with repentance.
No man of God is infallible; I apologise sincerely, Naomi.

FR FLYNN *bows towards* NAOMI. *SOGO and the priest stare down at* BONGINKOSI *and* NAOMI *in humility.* BONGINKOSI, *seeing the gravity of the matter, rises and offers a hand to* NAOMI. *She takes it and he pulls her to her feet.*

Sogo

Manoeuvred by demons I was indeed destructive.
In my voyage I was a glamorous clangouring catastrophe
Full of reason-abdicating obstinate devilish philosophy.
A twisted reverence of heaven was the vehement motive.
Demonically, the churches in their beauty reposed empty
While outside in howling wind and biting frost
The blind and the crippled huddled over papers for warmth
And luckless infants in gutters courted pneumonia
Said I to myself: This ungodly demagogic evil mania
Gratuitous and notorious to the suffering convert,
That preaches redemption while scalding believers' scalps,
Borne on gold-delighting sermons scaling the Alps,
From shameless lips Protestant, Presbyterian and Catholic
Gushing gospels of worldly wealth and earthly heaven,
And bodily health, had to be extinguished by flames of fire.

I burnt churches and mosques as a duty to the Almighty,

For in them I thought man was exalted, tithes idolised.

So, by my hand, the cathedral burned seven years ago.

NAOMI *sighs in relief and holds her chest.* SOGO *and* FR FLYNN *face the altar, genuflect thrice and stand still in a moment of reverence.* SOGO *gestures to* NAOMI *and* BONGINKOSI *to present themselves before the priest and altar. The two cross over and stand facing the robed men, between them the altar and the heap of items. Just then* VINCENT, *all along fidgeting with the radio set, switches it on, panics and jumps to his feet as the jingle for the South African Broadcasting Corporation News (SABC) shatters the silence at full volume, drawing everyone's attention.*

Radio

(*Female Sing-song Voice*)

Good afternoon listeners. In news just received from the Eastern Cape Province: an impromptu Eastern Cape Congress of Traditional Leaders of South Africa –CONTRALESA- conference held at the Meikles Hotel in Bisho this morning has conferred its five-yearly excellence award , the Chief Phalo Excellence Award, on *Sangoma* Sigcawu Mangcotywa of Nqadu Village for being true to his cause by discovering the site with a large body of underground water beneath it and establishing a shrine on it as a peg ahead of the recent discovery and intervention of the Ministry of Water Affairs and Forestry. The President of the Republic of South Africa, Mr Silvernos Molakeng, speaking at his Union Building Offices in Pretoria, wishes to congratulate *Sangoma* Sigcawu Mangcotywa for what he termed foresight and vision. The Chief Phalo Excellence Award is always accompanied by a kilogramme of refined gold among other lucrative benefits.

The all-Xhosa rainmaking shrine was for generations at the sacred Gxara River Pool, but upon the attainment of his mediumistic rainmaking tenure, *Sangoma* Sigcawu Mangcotywa exhumed ancestral relics from Gxara River Pool re-entombing them at Nqadu Village, which controversially became the new all-Xhosa rainmaking shrine. The *Sangoma* is still resident at the shrine and will be expected to relocate to pave way for the harvesting of the underground water. The Eastern Cape Provincial Government has agreed to purchase a farm in honour of the *Sangoma* in any place of his choice within their jurisdiction. Arrangements are under way for the National House of Traditional Leaders to present the Chief Phalo Excellence Award to the Eastern Cape *Sangoma* at a ceremony in Bisho within seven days. However, many members of CONTRALESA who boycotted this conference have vowed to strip *Sangoma* Sigcawu Mangcotywa of the award in a Court of Law.

Guiltily, VINCENT *bends and switches off the radio set and runs towards the nearest exit. Exit* VINCENT.

All are dumbfounded and exchange bewildered glances. BONGINKOSI *shrugs and spreads his arms in open wonder.* SOGO *shakes his head, crosses himself and lights the candlesticks using a cigarette lighter. Just then, faint wailing and shrieks emanate from the heap, prompting* BONGINKOSI *and* NAOMI *to cringe and step back in terror.* SOGO *quickly takes an unction bottle from the suitcase and gives it to* FR FLYNN, *who crosses himself thrice swiftly, opens the small bottle and sprinkles drops of water at the heap and at* BONGINKOSI *and* NAOMI *beyond it. As he sprinkles the water, he and* SOGO *loudly recite the Lord's Prayer in unison. Howling accompanies more wailing voices and shrieks coming from the heap, now visibly vibrating. The wailing increases to piercing screams akin to babies and women in agony. Plumes of smoke rise from the items.* NAOMI *and* BONGINKOSI *grimace as the crescendo builds, now from all directions in the homestead. Nondescript fetish items fall from the eaves of the consultation hut, some oozing blood, some smouldering. The plumes of smoke rising from the heap thicken and the noise of wailing voices and howling dogs builds to a deafening clangour.* NAOMI *and* BONGINKOSI *are visibly unnerved all the while, but* SOGO *and* FR FLYNN *remain bland and business-like, continuously reciting the Lord's Prayer and crossing themselves at the end of each recital. Their recital becomes spirited as the demonic crescendo builds.* NAOMI *grimaces and grabs* BONGINKOSI, *who quickly embraces her as they continue to inch backwards from the heap. Everywhere around the yard, gourds and more fetishes fall and, from the ground, dust swirls and rises. Overwhelmed,* NAOMI *clutches her chest, falls on the ground and lies still.*

Suddenly all the demonic noise and activity, except for the smouldering objects, dies, but SOGO *and* FR FLYNN *continue to recite the Lord's Prayer fervently.*

Enter two middle-aged rural men bearing the motionless figure of MANGCOTYWA *lying on a makeshift bier freshly made from poles and bark. A noose from straps of bark tightly cinctures* SANGOMA MANGCOTYWA'S *neck. The* SANGOMA'S *eyes are fixed and staring.* SOGO *and* FR FLYNN *fall silent upon seeing the copse and cross themselves. The pallbearers put down the corpse not far from the edge of the yard, murmur and click curses at the body, turn and quickly walk away. Exit the two men shaking their heads.*

FR FLYNN *and* SOGO *slowly cross over to inspect the body, while* BONGINKOSI *stoops over* NAOMI *and attempts to revive her.*

Final curtain

Appendice

APPENDIX I

Babylonian Talmud, Hagigah 14b

Passage

Our Rabbis taught: Four men entered an orchard and these are they: Ben Azzai, Ben Zoma, Aher and Rabbi Akiva. To them Rabbi Akiva said: "When you reach the stones of pure marble, do not say: 'Water, water!' For it is said: 'He that speaketh falsehood shall not be established before mine eyes'"[†]. Ben Azzai gazed and died. Of him scripture says: "Precious in the sight of the Lord is the death of his saints."[‡] Ben Zoma gazed and was stricken. Of him scripture says: "Hast thou found honey? Eat as much as is sufficient for thee, lest thou be filled therewith, and vomit it."[*] Aher cut down the shoots. Rabbi Akiva departed in peace.

[†] Psalms 101:7   [‡] Psalms 116:15   [*] Proverbs 25:16

Notes on the passage

- This famous passage of mystical experience, deliberated upon throughout the centuries as the major statement in rabbinic literature, has derivatives in the Tosefta, Hagigah 2: 1, 77a, and parallels in the Jerusalem Talmud, Hagigah 2: 3-4.
- All the four sages thrived in Persia in the first half of the second century. The passage is prefixed with the rabbinical formula: *Teno rabbanan*, meaning «Our Rabbis taught,» which always depicts the normal introduction of a *baraita* (i.e. a discourse from the era of *tannaim* and therefore not later than the end of the second century C.E.)
- The translation 'orchard' is from the Persian word *pardes* (literally orchard), occurring just once in the Bible (Song of Songs 4: 13). From this *pardes*, the

word 'paradise', standing for Heaven is derived. However, in the original passage we don't find the term *shamayyim* (heaven), but the usual term is *Gan Eden* (Garden of Eden). Therefore the famous interpretation of this passage is that the four did not ascend into Heaven but entered an earthly garden of a king, .i.e. the *pardes* / orchard of a king where they had to be circumspect and not venture into more private quarters of the property or wantonly cut down any shoots, destroying the fruit trees. In the final analysis, those who embark on the mystical ascent of the soul are compared to men entering a king's treasured orchard in which they are expected to practise caution or would risk punishment, at most execution.

- In Cabbala, this passage can be mystically interpreted to mean anything. In *Shrouded Blessings* it is fictionally and mystically, and engrossingly so, blended with a story to give a profoundly intriguing effect as the four sages are deliberately fused into one character (Bonginkosi), and one later becomes a modern Rabbi (Avuyah), and their singular entry into the orchard is changed to four independent numinous journeys undertaken by Bonginkosi.

Rabbi Aharon ben Shimon (PhD)
Centre for Jewish (Hasidic) Studies, Warsaw, 2009

APPENDIX II

National Anthem of South Africa

Nkosi Sikelel' iAfrica
Maluphakanyisw' uphondo Iwayo,
Yizwa imithandazo yethu,
Nkosi sikelela, thina lusapho Iwayo.

Morena boloka setjhaba sa heso,
O fedise dintwa la matshwenyeho,
O se boloke, O se boloke setjhaba sa heso,
Setjhaba sa South Africa – South Africa.

Uit die blou van onse hemel,
Uit die diepte van ons see,
Oor ons ewige gebergtes,
Waar die kranse antwoord gee.

Sounds the call to come together,
And united we shall stand,
Let us live and strive for freedom,
In South Africa, our land.

Courtesy of members of staff of the High Commission of South Africa in Harare, Zimbabwe (2009)

Authors's Notes
& Glossary

ACT ONE

SCENE I

Book of Ezekiel Ezekiel Chap I.

Pacer the Devil, Job 2:2

Areopagasus the hill of Ares in Athens, where the highest judicial council used   to meet, Acts 17:19.

Pegasus the Greek winged horse that erupted from the blood of Medusa.

Adonai Jewish for the Almighty

Primordial Drifter, Rover Spirit of God, Gen 1: 2

Peter Fonda a former Hollywood movie star

Qamata Xhosa for God

aBantu bomlambo calm human-like beings said to reside in rivers and the sea,   who admit into their family those who drown.

impundulu feared huge lightning birds

Lombardy East, Modderfontein western and eastern suburbs of Johannesburg

Emmarentia, Turffontein northern and southern suburbs of Johannesburg.

Horatio Hornblower novelist C.S Forester's machismo character

SCENE II

golem a giant Jewish automaton of clay, often in human form, believed to be   created by cabbalistic means and endowed with life.

Drankensberg a long range of high mountains in the Eastern Cape of South Africa.

right-hand son a Xhosa son of the Chief's second wife, who usually formed a   new clan within the tribe.

sangoma a South African diviner of great power.

MatsubayashiDance a Korean royal dance

tokoloshe a hairy and usually malevolent goblin that assumes many forms.

Memorare A Roman Catholic prayer

The Scorpions An elite unit within the South African police profoundly against fraud, tax evasion and corruption.

SCENE III

Athena a Greek goddess of wisdom and the arts of peace.

Poseidon, Apollo, Hephaestus Greek gods; ruler of the sea, god of the sun, music   and prophecy, and god of fire and metal work respectively.

Machinean pertaining to Manichaeism, a complicated religion founded by   Manes in Persia around 270AD, composed of elements of all religions Manes met (including Christianity). Almost all rulers (Christian and pagan)   persecuted Manichaeism as an enemy of mediaeval civilisation and morality.

ACT TWO

SCENE I

Jerusalem, Babylonian Talmud The Jerusalem (or Palestinian) Talmud mainly contains a compendium of discussions of the earliest codification of Jewish

Oral Law (*Mishnah*) by scholars and jurists in academies stretching over many centuries. The Babylonian Talmud incorporates the parallel intellectual discussions that went on in Babylonian academies.

Shaddai Jewish word in the Bible commonly translated 'Almighty'.

Johane Masowe an apostolic and prophetic sect founded by Sixpence Shonhiwa in Rhodesia (now Zimbabwe) in July 1932, averse to employment, education, the sturdy and reading of the Bible. He was later affectionately and spiritually known as Baba Johane (a corruption of John the Baptist). In 1947, fleeing possible detention emanating from his anti-European and anti-employment sermons, he and the inner core of his followers settled in Port Elizabeth in the Eastern Cape, where they sustained themselves through basket-weaving, the making of domestic tins and household furniture. By 1950 they were well-known as the Korsten Basket-makers and religiously as the Apostolic Sabbath Church of God or the vaHossana. In 1953 Baba Johane vainly applied to the Israeli Consul in South Africa for permission to relocate to Israel, where he intended to settle his members permanently as the chosen tribe of Israel. Unabated, the group began to trek northwards towards Israel by first moving to Marrapodi in Zambia where there promptly established an industrious Korsten. Baba Johane went further north, spending most of the 1960s secretly in Tanzania and Kenya in his efforts to chart a passage for his followers to Israel. In September 1973, at the time the church's 'Ark of the Covenant' was being transferred from Lusaka to Nairobi, Baba Johane returned to Zambia to die in a hospital in Ndola. His tomb is on top of Dandadzi Hill at Gandanzara, near Rusape in Zimbabwe. The tomb bears the simple engraving '*Ngirozi yeAfrica*' (Angel of Africa). Currently, the sect, whose members dress for church service typically in white toga-like garments, mainly flourishes in Zimbabwe, Botswana, South Africa, Zambia and some SADC countries, has not yet realised Baba Johane's wish to settle in Canaan.

Madzibaba reverent title or salutation for any male member of the *Johane   Masowe* apostolic sect.

egúngún an ancestral masquerade in Western Nigeria (Yoruba).

Oba, the title of a Yoruba Chief. ¥sÍ òkè very dear hand-woven cloth

iroko-tree African teak. *Òrò* a kind of tree demon / a secret and grim male cult that executes sentences of diviners.

aróso's wrapper wearer. *Orunmila*, the Yoruba omnilinguist divinity of divination said to understand every language spoken on earth, represents God's omniscience and knowledge and is famous for being a great   doctor.

iyan pounded yam.

àbikú in Yoruba community a demonic child which is born, dies, is born again and dies repeatedly like that.

babalawo oracular priest. *Ebon* sacrificial animal, usually a dog.

Shango the Yoruba god of thunder and lightning, representing God's wrath.

oogun grim supernatural juju.

Orinsa-nla regarded by the Yoruba as the 'supreme divinity' on the land, who deputises God on earth in creative and executive functions.

Ogun the Yoruba divinity for iron and war, originally believed to be a hunter or pathfinder who cleared the way for other divinities to land on earth.

SCENE II

Jo'burg Johannesburg

MaNdlovu wife of Mr Ndlovu or a woman of the Ndlovu (elephant) totem

SCENE IIII

Collegio Militare a building located about a kilometre from the Vatican. On the 10th October 1943, 365 soldiers of Hitler's SS troops entered Rome's old ghetto and arrested 1, 060 Italian Jews, whom they transported to this building, allegedly under the nose of Pope Pius XII. The Jews were detained in this building for two days before being loaded on cattle railroad trucks to Auschwitz where 80 percent of them were gassed within a week. The remainder became slave-labourers. 15 of the 1,060 survived the war.

ghommids wood spirits also believed to live in the ground.

Diabolosi Satan

ACT THREE

SCENE I

Itola the war medicine-men or doctor, who was responsible for the spiritual preparation of warriors before battle.

Nongqawuse a 14-year old Xhosa female *sangoma* who led her people (the Gcaleka tribe) to commit suicide. One day in 1856 she was looking down into a pool in the Gxara River when she alleged she saw the faces of her ancestors. The girl informed the Gcaleka (AmaXhosa) that the ancestors were willing and ready to drive the Europeans from their country. But foremost, to prove their belief in the ancestral spirits, the Xhosa would have to slaughter all their cattle and destroy all their crops. She threatened that those who refused would be turned into miserable creatures like frogs and mice and swept into the Indian Ocean by a ruthless whirlwind.

For ten months the Xhosa did as bidden, killing all their cattle and virtually destroying all their crops. The ancestors, she had said, would come on 18 February, 1857 to liberate the Xhosa. On that day, Nongqawuse predicted, a bloody, ochre-red sun would rise, stand still in the middle of the sky before setting again in the east. On that day nothing unusual happened in the sky or on the ground to the ruined expectant Xhosa. This fallacy saw about 25, 000 Xhosa people die of starvation. Those who survived did so through aid from surrounding tribes and the Europeans.

The Xhosa vied for Nongqawuse's blood, but she fled to a place in the King William's Town and found refuge with the British. Later she was kept for some time at Robben Island for her safety, but spent the rest of her life on a farm in the Eastern Province before passing away in 1898.

AmaRharhabe a separate branch of the Xhosa tribe formed by Rharhabe (1722-87), right-hand son of Chief Phalo, after a dispute arose between him and the heir-apparent, Gcaleka, eldest son of the Chief's first wife. Rharhabe was the eldest son of Chief Phalo's second wife.

red ochre the Xhosa smear their faces and bodies with red ochre when celebrating victory or any great achievement or occasion.

Nqadu Great Palace official residence of the king of the AmaXhosa (Gcaleka tribe) in the Eastern Cape, forty kilometres east of Idutywa, a small town en route to Mthatha.

Chief Phalo a great Chief of the Xhosa (1700-75) people of the Cape Province in now South Africa. He had two sons; Gcaleka (1730-92), who was the heir-apparent, and Rharhabe (1722-87), the right-hand son, who went on to form the AmaRharhabe tribe of the Xhosa by virtue of the right-hand son-ship. After the split, the people led by Gcaleka became known as the AmaXhosa.

SCENE II

Izikempe short stabbing spear with a broad blade for ripping, used at close quarters in battle.

Ijozi is like an *izikempe* spear only that the shaft is longer.

Gcau-u! A Xhosa, Zulu and Ndebele expression of anger or resentment

mpothulo in Xhosa culture, the bride takes three cows to the bridegroom's home. The first cow is the *impothulo*, which is slaughtered to feed the bridal party at a traditional wedding. *Inghakhwe* is the second cow that provides the bride with milk, symbolising her independence. *Ubulunga,* the third cow, is a sacred cow which isn't slaughtered, of which the wife has sole ownership. This cow, from the hairs of whose tail the wife makes a necklace to protect her and her children from evil, is never taken from her.

94lobola compulsory cattle (nowadays large sums of money) stipulated by future in-laws to a suitor to consummate a marriage.

Sakubona initial Zulu salutation for 'Greetings to you'.

CONRALESA Eastern Cape Congress of Traditional Leaders of South Africa.

impi a combative Zulu regiment for attacking.

SCENE III

shadoof a long wooden pole with a bucket on one end and a heavy weight on the other, for levering up water for irrigation in ancient times in Egypt, P a l e s t i n e and Syria. This old technology is still in use in some parts of North Africa and former Persia.

Alfasad a model of a hatchback car very popular in the 1980s.

Samye Temple a Tibetan Buddhist temple on a slope on the Himalayas.

Middle Way or the Majjhima Patipadâ given by the Buddha (by name Siddhartha Gautama, the son of the king of Kosala) in his First Sermon in India about 450 years before Christ, a teaching designed to render men desire-less of material things. It is the Noble Eightfold Path between all extremes (opposites) which leads to Enlightenment, a state of bliss, or tranquillity, or oneness with God, said to be possessed by all men and hidden in them, but attainable through concentration and meditation. The Buddha taught for over forty years before dying at Oudh in India.

Void or the sunya, a mind resting in the state of no-thinking. It is taught that a mind that reaches this state for a second or longer can understand the complete tranquillity and power that comes from Life (God within).

Fold the serene state of mind provided by adherence to the Eightfold Path for the attainment of the Void (Nirvana).

Mapungubwe Award highest honorary award in South Africa. Upon thepublication of this book its last recipient was Mr Jacob Zuma, then Chairman of the ANC, who was conferred with the award by the President of South Africa, His Excellence Mr Kcalema Motlante, a few minutes before the former was inaugurated as the new President of the Republic on 11, April 2009.

ACT FOUR

EPILOGUE

sensei a kung-fu or karate master of excellence who is so experienced in the art of fighting that he has surpassed supervision in his classes and at his tournaments.